W9-ASW-171

Lady, If You Go Into Politics: North Dakota's Women Legislators, 1923-1989

by
Ann M. Rathke

First Printing 1992

Copyright 1992
by
Sweetgrass Communications

ISBN 0-9632837-0-7

Published & Distributed by
Sweetgrass Communications
PO Box 3221
Bismarck, North Dakota
58502-3221

Table of Contents

List of Illustrations

List of Tables

To Rachel and the memory
of Larry

Acknowledgements

In mid-May 1988 I decided to take as my thesis topic a history of North Dakota's women legislators, a study that the North Dakota Council of Women Legislators had already raised the funds to publish. I came to that decision largely because of the encouragement of my husband, Larry Remele, who was historian/editor for the State Historical Society of North Dakota and a recognized authority on the state's political history. His rhetorical question—Do you know how many people would kill to have their thesis published?—was convincing. Knowing that I would have Larry's considerable expertise and wise counsel to draw on, I informed my thesis committee at the University of North Dakota History Department and the Council of Women Legislators of my decision. On June 3, 1988, Larry died. Though my interest in and commitment to the project was steadfast, my confidence that I could do it and do it well was not. Many people helped me regain that confidence and offered other invaluable help and support. I wish to thank them here.

I am grateful to my thesis committee, especially my advisor, Dr. Susan Peterson. I am pleased that I was able to complete my degree under Susan's guidance. Remaining committee members, Dr. Richard Beringer and Dr. D. Jerome Tweton of the UND History Department and Dr. James McKenzie of the UND English Department, offered valuable advice and criticism as well as timely support. With the assistance of my committee, in fall 1990 I completed my graduate work, a first and necessary step toward accomplishing this publication project.

Without the support and cooperation of the North Dakota Council of Women Legislators this book would not exist. During the 1987 Legislative Session women legislators organized with the purpose of publishing a history, a project for which they received sanctioning from the North Dakota Centennial Commission in 1989. They obtained funding for the publication from Northwestern Bell (now US West Communications). I am grateful to US West Communications for its financial support, and in particular to Jim DuBois, former Director of Public Affairs, for his early and consistent support, and to Lauren Stottler, Assistant Vice-president for Regulatory and Public Affairs, for enthusiastically embracing an inherited project.

I owe much to the fifty-seven former and current women legislators who contributed to this publication by completing an extensive survey, supplying newspaper clippings and other source material, and lending their encouragement. I am deeply indebted to Senator Corliss Mushik and Representative Brynhild Haugland, whose unfailing support included supplying me with personal photographs.

The work of transforming my thesis into a book was a time-consuming and painstaking process. I thank D. Jerome Tweton for his careful editing and Paula Tweton for her equally careful proofreading. My appreciation also goes to Everett Albers, Executive Director of the North Dakota Humanities Council, who administered project funds and facilitated the production of the book. I am grateful to George

Keiser and Sweetgrass Communications Inc. for seeing the value of this project and agreeing to take it on as one of their own.

Jerry Newborg and the staff of the State Historical Society of North Dakota Archives and Historical Research Library assisted in numerous ways. I am grateful to them, and in particular Todd Strand, who located and copied historic photographs. Mike Jacobs of the *Grand Forks Herald*, John Bye of the North Dakota Institute for Regional Studies, Sara Hanhan, and *The Bismarck Tribune* generously supplied other photographs. My thanks to them.

I also thank the following: Marilyn Guttromson and Audrey Sumner of the North Dakota Legislative Council Library for their assistance in locating and deciphering legislative records and their careful proofreading of the final manuscript; Sara Evans and Lloyd Omdahl for their insights; Kathie Anderson, Suezette Bieri, Julian Buxton, Janis Cheney, Scott Ellsworth, Jerry Hagstrom, John Hanson, Heidi Heitkamp, Thomasine Heitkamp, Lois Phillips Hudson, Mike Jacobs, Sharon Kessler, Carol Jean Larsen, Peg Michels, Alice Olson, J. Micheal McCormack, Louise Pare, and Bill Pratt for what each of them, in friendship, brought to me and to the project; Jeanne Ekart and Jan Joersz for many hours of child care; Leah Rogne for her unfailing support and good nature at all hours of the day and night; Diana Anderson, Janet Hranicky, and Gail Roen for helping me move through grief and toward joy; and Larry and Carole Woiwode for their loving encouragement.

Finally, and with affection, I thank my family for their steadfast support. My fondest appreciation goes to my daughter, Rachel Dakota Remele, whose belief in me and my work sustained me throughout this project. This book is dedicated to her and to the memory of Larry Rowen Remele.

Preface

Lady, if you go into politics, leave the men alone. Don't run to them for everything you want to know. Don't swallow all they tell you. Post yourself first, establish your own opinions—don't be a gull. Build your own knowledge and confidence—and do it by yourself.[1]

—Minnie D. Craig, 1933

In 1933 when Minnie Craig provided advice to women who were considering careers in politics, she was well qualified to speak on the subject. A veteran of six legislative sessions, she had been one of the state's first two female legislators and was now the first woman in any state to preside as Speaker of the House of Representatives. She was one of only 132 women who were serving in the nation's state legislatures.[2]

Politics in general and state legislatures in particular have historically been the province of men. "Political man"

13

has been well documented. "Political woman," long considered a contradiction in terms, has until recent years scarcely been noted. This book, which is a collective biography of North Dakota's women legislators, adds a new chapter to the growing body of literature about women in American politics.

Little is known about the seventy-two women who served in the North Dakota legislature between 1923, when women first took seats, and 1989, the state's Centennial year.[3] Collectively and individually they go unmentioned in the major histories of the state, including Elwyn Robinson's *History of North Dakota* (1966), a standard by which other histories are measured. Even Minnie Craig, a "first" in the state and the nation, does not make so much as a footnote in Robinson's study. Lack of knowledge of the history of these few, but important women has resulted in the spread of misinformation about them. For example, when Shirley Lee was named Outstanding Legislator of the Year by the National Republican Legislators Association in 1984, press coverage of her award referred to her as "the first woman chairman of a Senate standing committee."[4] In fact, Lee was the third, not the first, woman to chair such a committee. The purpose of this book is to remedy this lack of information and to paint a group portrait of seventy-two women who forged a particular place for themselves in North Dakota's unique and colorful political heritage. How they forged that place and how, in the 1980s, they came of age with the knowledge and confidence envisioned by Minnie Craig in 1933 are central issues in the collective story of these women.

Each chapter is organized around a series of questions. Who were these few women who sought and won legislative positions during North Dakota's first one hundred years of statehood? What were their collective and individual backgrounds and subsequent pathways to the legislature? What were their major legislative interests and how were these reflected in their committee assignments? What committee chairs and other leadership positions did they hold? What were their legislative initiatives, particularly those on behalf of women? And finally, how did the answers to these questions change over time?

Information for this study came from a variety of sources, including surveys completed from March to October 1989 by fifty-seven former and current women legislators; archival and newspaper collections held by the State Historical Society of North Dakota and the North Dakota Institute for Regional Studies; newspaper clippings in the libraries of the *Grand Forks Herald*, *The Bismarck Tribune*, and the *Fargo Forum*; legislative records held by the North Dakota Legislative Council; and interviews with former and current women legislators and their relatives. Numerous books and articles about women in national, state, and local politics, including the few but invaluable studies of the role of women in North Dakota's political tradition, provided background material as well as a focus for the work.

This collective biography is divided into three time periods, 1923 to 1969, 1970 to 1979, and 1980 to 1989. The twenty women who served in the legislature between 1923 and 1969 are the subject of chapter 1. Chapter 2 focuses on the thirty-one women who served in the legislature in the 1970s. Twenty-six of these women began their service in the Seventies and five were veteran legislators from the previous period. The subject of chapter 3 is the forty-one women who served in the legislature in the 1980s. Of this group of women, twenty-six began their service in the Eighties and fifteen carried over from previous periods. The changing profile of North Dakota's women legislators unfolds throughout the course of these three chapters. Chapter 4 summarizes these changes in a brief conclusion.

Preface End Notes

[1]"TRUST IN SELF, SAYS SPEAKER: Minnie Craig Gives Advice to Women Considering Politics," *Fargo Forum*, [February 1933], Minnie Craig Scrapbook, Minnie D. Craig Papers, North Dakota Institute for Regional Studies, North Dakota State University, Fargo.

[2]"132 WOMEN ARE IN STATE LEGISLATURES: Won Elections in 34 States—Mrs. Minnie D. Craig Speaker of N.D. House," *Valley City Peoples Opinion*, 12 January 1933, Minnie Craig Scrapbook

[3]North Dakota's women legislators are listed in alphabetical order in appendix A. Selected details of their service are provided. Appendix B lists women legislators by session.

[4]"State legislator honored," *Bismarck Tribune*, 2 August 1984.

1

Politics, Still A Man's World: The 1920s through the 1960s

Masculine hostility to the idea of women having an equal share in the privileges and responsibilities of government did not melt away after ratification of the Nineteenth Amendment which granted them the vote. After more than thirty years, politics is still a man's world. India Edwards, Vice-Chairman of the Democratic National Committee, summed up the tribulations of a woman politician in one exasperated comment, "If I didn't have the crusading spirit, I'd get the hell out and go home."[1]

—Eleanor Roosevelt and Lorena A. Hickok, 1954

*Women have much to learn in the "Game of Government." Men have been **the** politicians for so long, they much resent the interference of women upon their exclusive right to handle the cash, line up all the scemes [sic], tell everyone what they must do and be very careful not to tell them "Why."[2]*

—Minnie D. Craig, [1954-1956]

Politics for women in North Dakota, or anywhere else, is no pink-tea affair.[3]

—Brynhild Haugland, [1950]

Historical Background and Overview

Women's participation in the "game of government" began long before ratification of the Nineteenth Amendment to the United States Constitution on August 26, 1920. Barred from the electoral arena of voting and office holding, women learned to play and even influence the game from the outside. Through their clubs and other voluntary associations, women worked collectively to create and demand change in government institutions and public policy.[4]

Elizabeth Preston Anderson of Fargo was a leading suffragist. Credit: North Dakota Institute for Regional Studies

In North Dakota the female voice for change and reform from territorial days through the first two decades of the twentieth century focused primarily on the issues of temperance and woman suffrage. For many women, including Elizabeth Preston

18

Anderson of Fargo, female suffrage was a means to attain social goals, particularly prohibition.[5] Anderson was a leader in both the temperance and woman suffrage movements.

The women of Dakota Territory had gained limited suffrage before statehood in 1889, with the right to vote in local school elections and for state superintendent of public instruction and county superintendent. In 1917 woman suffrage was expanded in North Dakota to include voting in municipal and presidential elections.[6] Apparently unable or unwilling to integrate fully these new voters into the election process, poll officials required women to use separate ballot boxes in the presidential election of 1918.[7]

Described as a "long, exhausting battle,"[8] the struggle for woman suffrage in North Dakota was waged primarily in the legislative chambers. Suffragists endured more than one "defeat by political trickery"[9] at the hands of opponents in the legislature. On the last day of the 1893 session, for example, a woman suffrage bill, which Senator James W. Stevens of Dickey County had introduced, passed the Senate and was sent to the House. After Elizabeth Preston Anderson addressed the House, the chamber passed the bill. According to Anderson,

"Following the vote came a most spectacular fight. The Speaker of the House, George Walsh, refused to sign the bill. Governor Shortridge, however, said the bill did not need the speaker's signature and that he would sign it if it reached his office. For many hours after that, however, the bill was mysteriously lost and men were placed in the halls to prevent it from reaching the governor's office. It never did".[10]

Final victory for female suffrage came as a result of the Nineteenth Amendment, ratified in North Dakota on December 2, 1919, in a special session of the legislature.[11] In addition to full voting rights, ratification of the Nineteenth

Amendment meant expanded opportunities for women to seek elective office. Up until this time only three women had sought and won statewide office in North Dakota, all in the position of superintendent of public instruction.[12]

With the door open for full political participation by women, suffragists and anti-suffragists alike predicted the rise of a female voting bloc poised to transform American life and politics, for better or for worse. Recognizing this potential, politicians turned their attention to women voters and sought to win their support. The first half of the 1920s witnessed a flurry of legislation in Congress and in legislatures across the country, addressing the special interests of women.[13]

In 1987 Brynhild Haugland was honored as the longest serving state legislator in the nation. Credit: The Bismarck Tribune

Although women did exhibit certain patterns of political participation different from men, including lower voter turnout, clearly by the end of the 1920s a women's bloc did not exist. Legislators became less responsive to questions perceived as women's issues. Women continued to be vastly outnumbered by men in public office, as women and men alike continued to view politics as a "man's world."[14] The door to political power and equality that suffragists had predicted would open for women was only slightly ajar.

Against this historical backdrop women began to seek and win seats in North Dakota's legislature. Two women were elected in 1922 in the first state election after full woman suffrage. From the 1923 session through the 1969 session, twenty women served in the legislature, eighteen in the House and two in the Senate.[15]

Of the women who entered legislative service during this forty-six year period, eleven, or just over half, served a single term. Five women served between two and five terms and four served six or more. One explanation for the significant number of short-term female legislators is that women entered politics to champion issues not to pursue professions.[16] A striking exception to this pattern is Brynhild Haugland of Minot, who won election to the House in 1939. In 1989 she served her twenty-sixth term as a representative. Two years earlier she was recognized and honored as the nation's longest serving state lawmaker.[17] Her tenure was so unusual for the era that as early as 1951 Brynhild Haugland was being referred to as "a long term lady legislator."[18]

All but three of the women who began their legislative tenure before 1970 were the first women from their respective counties to serve in the North Dakota legislature. Fourteen (70 percent) of the twenty women were elected from counties east of a line dividing North Dakota in half east to west (see figure 1). Three counties—Cass, Ward, and Pierce—sent more than one woman to the legislature. People in the

Fig 1. Post offices of women legislators serving between 1923 and 1969. (Base map: North Dakota Highway Department.)

counties west of the Missouri River elected no women. Six women were elected out of three of the state's four most populated cities—Fargo, Minot, and Grand Forks. The remaining fourteen came from small towns and rural areas.

The largest number of women to serve in any one session were the five who served in 1967. They held just over 3 percent of the legislative seats. Fourteen, or over two-thirds, served at least one session as the lone woman in a chamber or with one other woman. Brynhild Haugland was the sole woman in the entire legislature for four sessions and the only woman in the House for an equal number of sessions. Only the 1935 session had no women.

When North Dakota's premier women legislators, Minnie Craig of Esmond and Nellie Dougherty of Minot, took their places in the House of Representatives in January of 1923, North Dakota was suffering an economic depression caused by low crop prices and poor crops. The post-war prosperity that most of the nation enjoyed bypassed North Dakota. The end of free land and the beginning of a rural exodus signaled the passing of the pioneer era.[19]

Five women served in the 1967 legislative session. They were (left to right) Aloha Eagles, Grace Stone, Fern Lee, Brynhild Haugland, and Helen Claire Ferguson. Courtesy: Brynhild Haugland

North Dakota politics in the 1920s reflected not only the economic depression of the state but also the political movements afoot in the nation. The Nonpartisan League (NPL), called "North Dakota's greatest political insurgency,"[20] and the Independent Voters' Association (IVA), an organization formed in reaction to the League, struggled to control the Republican Party and state government.[21] Organized in 1915 by Arthur C. Townley, the League fought for progressive reforms such as state ownership of banks, mills, and elevators. The IVA attacked the League with charges that NPL leaders were socialistic and anti-American. Minnie Craig, a Leaguer, and Nellie Dougherty, a Democrat whom the Independents employed and supported, represented the two warring factions of the dominant Republican Party.

The 1930s was a period of explosive politics which saw the removal of William Langer as governor in July 1934 and

Minnie Craig of Esmond (left) and Nellie Dougherty of Minot were North Dakota's first women legislators. Credit: State Historical Society of North Dakota

a succession of four governors in the seven months between July 1934 and February 1935. A new anti-League faction, the Republican Organizing Committee (ROC), came to power in the 1940s. The success of the ROC forced the Nonpartisan League and the Democratic party to join forces in the 1950s. In 1960 they merged to create the new Democratic-Nonpartisan League.[22]

Women legislators' party loyalties continued to reflect the dominant political culture. Seventeen (85 percent) of the first twenty women lawmakers were aligned with either League or IVA Republicans. Only after the League united with the Democratic party in the mid-1950s and a healthy two-party system took root in North Dakota did Democratic women begin to seek and win legislative seats in more than minuscule numbers.

Background Characteristics

Outlining and comparing the background characteristics of North Dakota's women legislators over time is essential to determine changes in their collective history and profile in the sixty-six years covered in this study. According to Irwin N. Gertzog, author of *Congressional Women: Their Recruitment, Treatment, and Behavior*, documented change in background characteristics "means that there has been change in the social, economic, and political resources that successful female candidates have been able to aggregate and exploit."[23] In this and the following two chapters these background characteristics will be traced and analyzed: age, marital status, number and age of children, and occupation at the time of first election to the legislature; education; ethnic background and religious preference; prior political experience and family political connections; and political party and organizational affiliations.

Biographical information about the twenty women who served in the legislature between 1923 and 1969 is extensive, but by no means complete. A major source of this information is contemporary newspapers. The press, and presumably the public, showed more than a passing interest in the professional and personal backgrounds of the state's early women legislators.

An example of this interest is the press reaction which greeted Minnie Craig and Nellie Dougherty at the commencement of the 1923 legislative session. The *Fargo Forum* reported that both Craig and Dougherty had taught school, disliked publicity, believed in economy and cooperation, and expected to support the programs of their respective factions.[24] The same newspaper noted that Craig was "a musician of ability and a good cook according to her friends."[25] John Andrews, editor of the *Courier-News* at Fargo, described Craig as "a fine clear-eyed and clear-thinking woman of good presence and attractive personality" and Dougherty as "a slight slip of womanhood, youthful and obviously earnest." Andrews apparently deduced Dougherty's earnest nature when at the swearing in ceremony "her white face set out in profile and her lips moving gave the impression of a young girl at prayer."[26] Though earnestness and musical and culinary abilities are not among the background characteristics to be discussed in this study, other characteristics deemed noteworthy by the contemporary press, such as occupation and political party affiliation, will be.

The first woman to gain a legislative seat via the "widow's route" was Rosamund O'Brien of Park River. Credit: State Historical Society of North Dakota

Age, Marital Status, and Number and Age of Children at Time of First Election to the Legislature

Women officeholders tend to be middle-aged[27] and to seek and obtain public office at a later age than men.[28] Traditional women's roles, particularly child rearing, have been cited as a possible explanation for this pattern.[29]

From 1923 to 1969 the median age of the twenty first-term North Dakota women legislators was forty-eight. Upon their election, they ranged in age from thirty-three to sixty-two. The youngest were Nellie Dougherty, elected in 1922, and Brynhild Haugland, elected in 1938. Both were thirty-three when first elected. Dougherty was the youngest member of the House in the 1923 session.[30] The oldest woman was Sybil Kelly, elected in 1958 at age sixty-two. Three-fourths, or fifteen, of the women were in their forties and fifties at the time of their initial election.

Popular images of the woman officeholder include widows who succeeded husbands who died in office, divorcees whose marriages could not withstand the demands of public life, and single career women without family constraints.[31] In fact, the marital profile of North Dakota's first twenty women legislators shows little resemblance to this popular image. Five (25 percent) were single upon election. Fourteen were married, one was widowed, and none were divorced. This profile would have surprised Illinois legislator Bernice T. Van Der Vries, who in 1948 observed that "so many of the women winning public office are widows, with a minimum of home responsibilities."[32]

If the term "widow's succession" is interpreted broadly, one woman could be said to have entered the legislature via this route. In 1951 Senator Harry O'Brien of Park River, who had served three terms in the House and three terms in the Senate, announced his retirement due to ill health and "hinted he would like to see Mrs. O'Brien chosen for the post which he proposed to vacate."[33] He subsequently "brought the matter up"[34] at the county Democratic nominating convention the following year and Rosamund O'Brien was nominated for the post. Mrs. O'Brien was elected by a comfortable margin in the November election and served her first session in 1953. Harry O'Brien died on October 10, 1953.[35]

Whether it is manageable, appropriate, or even moral for a woman to seek and hold public office when she has young children has been an issue of long-standing debate. In her study of women legislators in 1974, Jeane J. Kirkpatrick observed that society prescribes a clear hierarchy of values for women—children first, husbands second, careers last. According to Kirkpatrick, many of the women in her study avoided a conflict around this prescription by delaying legislative service until their children were grown or at least well beyond what might be considered a tender age.[36]

Given the role constraints experienced and described by a representative sampling of female lawmakers in the mid-1970s, it is not surprising that forty years earlier pioneer woman legislator Minnie Craig contended that the only woman who did not belong in politics was the mother of young children. Married and childless, Craig declared that, "If I had young children, you'd not find me here. I'd be home where I would belong."[37] Agnes Geelan of Enderlin, whose long political career boasted several firsts, including North Dakota's first woman mayor (elected in 1946 and 1950) and first female state senator (elected in 1950 and 1952), believed that having a supportive husband and no children gave her the freedom to pursue her career. Speaking to a reporter in 1982, Geelan stated that had she had children, "You wouldn't be talking to me today."[38]

Of the twenty women who served in the legislature between 1923 and 1969, five (25 percent) were single women with no children. Of the fifteen married women, three had no children, although one, Rosamund O'Brien of Park River,

Lavina Amsberry of Wheelock and Mabel Lindgren of Minot were the first mothers to serve in the legislature. Credit: State Historical Society of North Dakota

was a foster mother. Seven of the married women with children were first elected to the legislature after their children were eighteen or over. These fifteen women fit the profile of the "typical" woman officeholder with no active child rearing responsibilities.

Five married women legislators sought and won election when they had at least one child under eighteen. Lavina Amsberry of Wheelock and Mabel Lindgren of Minot, elected in 1928, were the first mothers in the legislature. Amsberry's area newspaper recognized her distinction with a headline reading "The First Mother of Our District in the Legislature."[39] She had two children at home, ages eleven and fifteen.[40] Mabel Lindgren's five children were between the ages of seventeen and six.[41] Pregnant with her sixth child,

Lindgren decided not to seek reelection in 1930.[42] Two women with children at home were in the legislature in the 1930s—Nellie Olson of Wilton with one child in elementary school and another in high school[43] and Susie Ista of Walcott with four children between the ages of seventeen and five.[44] Not until 1966 was another mother of a school age child, Helen Claire Ferguson of Rugby, elected to the legislature. All five of the women with one or more children at home were one-term legislators.

Occupation When First Elected to the Legislature and Educational Background

Politics differs from most professions in that participation, even as an officeholder, requires no specific educational or occupational training. Minimum requirements for public office seekers relate to citizenship, age, and residence, not education or occupation. Even so, officeholders as a rule have higher educational and professional status than the general population.[45] Of the professions, law is traditionally the most common among officeholders. Legal knowledge and skills have been seen as assets to both the political candidate and the public officeholder.[46]

Although little national research was conducted on the educational and occupational backgrounds of women state legislators before 1970, a 1968 study provided the following profile of women in the 1963/64 state legislatures. While most had some post-high school education, less than half were college graduates. Most had worked in one or more professions, with business, public relations, and teaching the most common. Represented, but less well, were the mass media, law, social work, and nursing. Farmers, doctors, and ministers were few and far between.[47] A profile of women holding office, including legislative seats, during 1974 and 1975 indicates a predominance of traditional women's occupations. Poorly represented were occupations such as "law, journalism, public administration or insurance and real

30

estate, which are frequently associated with political activity and entry into office."[48]

North Dakota's first twenty women legislators ranged in educational background from some high school training to a graduate degree, with a majority having had some post-

Though a majority of North Dakota of North Dakota's early women legislators were college graduates, only one, Helen Claire Ferguson of Rugby, had a masters degree. Credit: State Historical Society of North Dakota

high school education. Seven (35 percent) attended or completed high school; thirteen (65 percent) attended or completed college. Of the thirteen women in the latter group, two had some college training and eleven were college graduates. While three of these college graduates did post-graduate work, only one of the state's pioneer women legislators earned a post-graduate degree. She was Helen Claire Ferguson, who had a master's degree in institutional management. Six of the college-educated women graduated from normal or teachers colleges and one from a business college. The first five women in the legislature were normal school graduates.

While the educational profile of North Dakota's early women legislators is quite typical of female officeholders in general, their occupational profile is less so. Although seven, or just over one-third, of the women who served in the legislature between 1923 and 1969 taught school before their legislative service, none were teachers at the time they were elected. In general, traditional female occupations were not well represented among this group of women. The occupations of nursing and social work were absent. Only one woman, Nellie Dougherty, was employed in a clerical position. Four women were full-time homemakers when they entered the legislature. Eleven combined homemaking responsibilities with employment outside the home.

Most of the early women legislators who were employed outside the home were engaged in nontraditional occupations, including farming, insurance, banking, sales, and journalism. Farmers and journalists were particularly well represented among this group of women, with six women engaged in farming and three employed in newspaper work. While several of North Dakota's first women legislators were engaged in one of the occupations traditionally associated with political activity and advancement, none were employed in that occupation most associated with politics—law.

Ethnic Background and Religious Preference

In the preface to *Plains Folk: North Dakota's Ethnic History* (1988) sociologist and ethnic scholar William C. Sherman weighs the importance of ethnicity or nationality in the state's history. "In a sense," he wrote, "the story of the ethnic groups in North Dakota *is* the story of North Dakota." Scholars and nonscholars alike have long recognized that ethnic background influences the way that many of us live our daily lives. The ethnic component can figure into matters as mundane as food and beverage tastes and as important as job preference and work habits, level of education and educational performance, and religious and political behavior.[49]

When women began to serve in the state legislature in the 1920s, North Dakota was a land of immigrants. A majority of the state's population was foreign-born or had at least one parent who was foreign-born. Nationality groups continued to cluster in self-defined communities well into the 1950s. Ethnic identification remains strong in North Dakota, particularly in the rural areas. Ethnic diversity is also a persistent theme.[50]

Information about the ethnic backgrounds of seventeen of the state's first twenty female legislators is available. Seven (41 percent) had at least one parent of British Isles ancestry, including English, Scotch, Scotch-Irish, and Irish. Familiar with government by tradition, individuals of British Isles descent dominated the state's politics for several decades after statehood in 1889. Most notable was Alexander McKenzie, the "Boss of North Dakota" and a Canadian Scot.[51] Four (24 percent) of the seventeen women were of German descent by virtue of one or both parents. Germans from Russia, the second largest nationality group in the state, were not represented.[52]

Nine (53 percent) women legislators claimed one or both parents of Scandinavian ancestry, including Norwegians, Danes, and Swedes. Over half of these women descended from Norwegians, the largest nationality group in North Dakota. Described as "politically restless," Norwegian Americans have generally been aggressive in seeking public office and exerting political influence. Temperance was one cause for which many Norwegian North Dakotans crusaded.[53]

The ethnic heritage of the women who began their legislative service between 1923 and 1969 is clearly not as diverse as North Dakota's general population, which also includes Ukrainians, Poles, Czechs, Bulgarians, French, Syrians, Dutch, Belgians, and others. Only one woman, Grace Stone of Grand Forks, drew her lineage from one of these groups, in this case the French.

Religious preference and ethnic background are biographical variables which are often linked. Scandinavians, for example, are traditionally Lutherans.[54] One might expect that the strong showing of Scandinavian women in the legislature between 1923 and 1969 would mean a healthy percentage of the women would be Lutheran. This expectation is born out. More women are identified as Lutheran (six, or 30 percent) than any other single denomination.

Nine other women belonged to other Protestant denominations, including Congregational, Methodist, Presbyterian, Episcopal, and Moravian. The total percentage of Protestant women is fifteen. Three women (15 percent) are identified as Catholic. One woman identified herself as a Christian and another·indicated no religious preference.

Family Political Connections and Prior Political Experience

In his study of the first one hundred female U.S. Congresswomen, Irwin Gertzog observes that many of these women had a parent or other close relative who had held public office. Before World War II family political connections, combined with family wealth, "were virtually indis-

34

pensable to would-be congresswomen." Women who are exposed to political activism in their developmental years are presumed to be less influenced or constrained by societal prescriptions regarding the world of politics, which traditionally has been a male world.[55]

According to Gertzog, prior political experience in elective or appointive office and in political party leadership provides "would-be representatives with the appropriate skills, political orientations, proximity to decision-making centers, visibility, and credibility."[56] Although generaliza-

Agnes Geelan was mayor of Enderlin when she was first elected to the legislature in 1950. Credit: State Historical Society of North Dakota

tions about the previous political experience of female state legislators who held seats before 1970 are not available, one scholar observed that women in the 1963/64 state legislatures commonly served in state or local party organizations or in municipal government before their election to the legislature.[57] A study of women who held office on all levels during 1974 and 1975 revealed that "sizeable percentages of women" had previous office-holding experience.[58]

Prior political experience was also common among North Dakota's early women legislators. Eight (40 percent) sought and won public office before their legislative career. Of these women all but one served on a county or city school board or as county superintendent of schools. One in this group of women, Agnes Geelan, was a mayor when first elected to the legislature.

Activism in the county or local school district was a common and perhaps predictable political training ground for women during this period. In 1929 *The Bismarck Tribune* reported that first-term legislator Lavina Amsberry's training for politics was obtained working for the division of school districts in her county. All but one of the eight women with prior political experience had been a school board member or a superintendent of schools before becoming a legislator. The sole exception was Mabel Lindgren, who served one term as a justice of the peace in Minot before entering the legislature.[59]

At least half of the women who entered the legislature before 1970 were active in precinct, district, or state political party organizations before becoming legislators. Eight of the first twelve women legislators belonged to the Nonpartisan League, which had a large, active women's membership from its beginning.[60] In 1919 Minnie Craig was elected president of the League's network of women's clubs. On the opposite side of the political fence, Nellie Dougherty became interested and active in politics while working as a stenographer at the Independent Voters Association headquarters in Minot.[61] Beginning in the 1950s and throughout the 1960s, it was common for a female legislator to have served as a precinct committee chair and/or on one or more campaign committees before becoming a successful legislative candidate.

Family political connections were also an integral part of the profile of the state's pioneer women legislators. Nearly half of these women claimed family roots in electoral politics. The most common family link was a father or husband who had served in public office at some point before the woman's legislative service. John Sanderson, father of

Five of North Dakota's early women legislators, including Laura Sanderson of LaMoure, followed in their fathers' footsteps when they sought and won public office. Credit: State Historical Society of North Dakota

Laura Sanderson of LaMoure, was an early county judge and a city council member. John McGinnis, father of Mary McGinnis of Jamestown, became a city alderman in 1883. Henry Ellingson, father of Nettie Ellingson of Rugby, served several terms as register of deeds for Pierce County, and Helen Claire Ferguson's father was a state's attorney. Grace Stone's husband was on the Grand Forks board of education before her bid for a legislative seat.

Rosamund O'Brien, Sybil Kelly, and Anna Powers had an immediate family member or an in-law who preceded them in the legislature. Kelly's father, Fred Baker, served in the Senate from 1909 to 1912, and O'Brien's husband, Harry O'Brien, served in the House from 1934 to 1940 and in the Senate from 1940 to 1952. Anna Powers' father-in-law served in the House during the 1905 and 1907 sessions.

Early women legislators expressed a sense of inherited political interest and activism. Mabel Lindgren, who served in the 1929 session, told a reporter that she had inherited her interest in politics from her politically active father and that "questions of the day were discussed at home."[62] While growing up, Mary Rathbun of Crystal, elected in 1932, was exposed to conversations "centered on government and politics, economics, and social changes needed to improve living conditions."[63] Three-term House member Sybil Kelly of Devils Lake observed, "It seems as though I've heard about politics all my life."[64]

Organizational Affiliations

Previous political experience and family political connections have long been viewed as distinct advantages on the path to public office. Organizational activity is yet another means of developing the political awareness, knowledge, and skills that are often seen as prerequisites for office-holding. Because women's organizations have served as leadership-training grounds for women since before female suffrage and because women have traditionally been less involved in professions, such as law, which are associated with office-holding, organizational affiliation is likely to be especially important to women office seekers.[65] Joanne V. Hawks, who

The League of Women Voters prepared many women, including Aloha Eagles of Fargo, for future public office. Credit: State Historical Society of North Dakota

has authored or coauthored a number of articles about women legislators in southern states, notes "the frequent presence of the so-called clubwoman in politics."[66]

Clubwomen abound among the first twenty women to serve in the North Dakota legislature. All of these women were members of at least one organization and most held memberships in three or more groups. A wide range of organizations are represented, including political, professional, public service and affairs, religious, farm, social and cultural, sororial, and patriotic. The General Federation of Women's Clubs and local women's clubs were particularly popular.

Membership in a women's auxiliary of a political party or faction, such as the Nonpartisan League Women's Clubs and county and state Republican women's clubs, was common. Activism and leadership in nonpartisan women's political organizations such as the League of Women Voters have often served women as a route to state legislatures. Organized nationally in 1920, the League of Women Voters has been referred to as "a kind of farm club for women politicians."[67] Aloha Eagles, first elected in 1966, gives the League of Women Voters total credit for her successful bid for a House seat.[68] In the 1970s the League of Women Voters route to the legislature would be increasingly prevalent.

Legislative Interests

An officeholder's background characteristics, from education and occupation to political and organizational affiliations, influence what interests he or she brings to and develops in office. The interests of women officials are a topic of long-standing discussion. The debate over women's suffrage extended to the question of what interests and concerns women would pursue once they had the right to seek and hold public office. Would they, for example, follow the lead of Congresswoman Jeannette Rankin of Montana and "infect politics with pacifism" as some feared?[69]

Education, health, welfare, and children are foremost among those policy areas that are of special interest to female legislators. Women's prelegislative experiences as wives and mothers and in "feminine" occupations such as teaching, nursing, and social work have explained this pattern.[70] Inter-

40

ests that are regarded as traditionally female are accorded lower status than traditionally male interests, which center around finance.[71]

Between 1923 and 1969 North Dakota's women legislators most commonly shared an interest in education. Sybil Kelly spoke for other early women legislators when in 1959

Education, traditionally a major legislative priority of women lawmakers, was a special interest of Sybil Kelly of Devils Lake. Credit: State Historical Society of North Dakota

as a first-term representative she stated, "Education has always been one of my special interests."[72]

The women legislators also shared a common concern for welfare of people, especially women and children and the elderly. During her first term in the House in 1923 Minnie Craig "declared that she was deeply interested in all legislation affecting women and children."[73] Craig's focus on women went beyond their general welfare to issues of women's rights. Emphasis upon women's rights among the state's women legislators received new life in the 1960s with the election of women such as Representative Aloha Eagles of Fargo who championed such issues as the Equal Rights Amendment.[74] Lavina Amsberry, elected in 1928 and familiar herself with the "patterns of a farm woman's life," emphasized the welfare of rural women.[75]

A few women held special interest in health care and law enforcement. Individual women focused their attentions on a variety of topics such as taxes, the judiciary, transportation, government improvement, revision of election laws, labor relations, the environment, safety, agriculture, water programs, zoning, municipal government, and tourism. This indicates that while North Dakota's early women legislators did show significant interest in education and welfare, their legislative interests were wide ranging.

Committee Assignments

According to Jeane J. Kirkpatrick in *Political Woman*, committee assignments reflect a legislator's special interests. Commonly, the committee assignment process begins when legislators submit their preferences to the leadership of their respective houses at the start of each session. These requests are generally honored.[76] In North Dakota the Speaker of the House makes committee appointments after consulting with party floor leaders. In the Senate the committee on committees makes these appointments.[77] Because much of the important work of the legislature is done in committees, committee assignments are taken seriously by those who give them and those who get them. A legislator's committee assignments have a direct influence upon which policy areas that legislator will concentrate.[78]

Comparative studies of state legislatures have shown that when committee assignments are doled out, ". . . women are more likely to be assigned to committees such as Education, Health, and Welfare; whereas men are more likely to be assigned to Appropriations, the Judiciary, and other committees dealing with money and capital development."[79] Other related committees typically assigned to women are those concerned with disadvantaged groups, local government, government ethics, and various "housekeeping" details necessary to the smooth operation of the legislative body itself. Until the 1960s women's service on congressional committees showed a similar pattern, with congresswomen generally receiving initial and subsequent committee assignments deemed appropriate to their gender.[80]

In her 1974 study of women legislators, Jeane J. Kirkpatrick advanced two possible explanations for this pattern. First,

"the male leaders of party and legislature—and the leaders are male—discriminate against women in making committee and subcommittee assignments, systematically excluding them from the powerful committees, and shunting them, regardless of their interest and preferences, onto the 'poor' committees desired by no one because they influence nothing or, at best, to those committees whose subject matter is presumed (by these same males) to be especially suited to women."[81]

Second, women are concentrated on education, welfare, and health committees because these are policy areas in which they have a special interest and are inclined to request.

43

Although Kirkpatrick favored the latter explanation, both explanations have their proponents.[82] Available data are insufficient to draw conclusions about the experience of North Dakota's women legislators in regard to this question. However, it is possible to demonstrate the extent to which these women have focused, by virtue of their committee assignments, on "male" versus "female" policy domains.

When women began to serve in the North Dakota legislature in 1923, there were thirty-one standing committees in the House and Senate. The titles and number of standing committees fluctuated slightly over the next two decades. With the establishment of the Legislative Research Committee in 1945,[83] the standing committees were reorganized. In 1947 the number of standing committees was reduced to fourteen.[84] This and several other modernizing measures produced an orderly committee system in which, according to long-term legislator Brynhild Haugland, "All new legislators have an opportunity to serve on important committees."[85] In 1971 the number of standing committees was further reduced to twelve, including one joint committee.[86] The discussion of committee assignments in this chapter falls into two periods, 1923 to 1946 and 1947 to 1969.

Between the 1923 session and the 1947 session ten women were in the legislature. These women were assigned to and served on twenty-three committees. They typically held seats on at least three committees. Their assignments were concentrated in Education (eight women or 80 percent), Temperance (eight women or 80 percent), Public Health (five women or 50 percent), Apportionment (four women or 40 percent), and Revisions and Corrections of the Journal (four women or 40 percent). Minnie Craig referred to this last committee as "a sort of 'waste basket' into which new members might be tossed so that they would think they had a 'committee appointment.' "[87] When Social Welfare was created in 1939, the only two women legislators (Brynhild

44

Haugland and Susie Ista) were assigned to the committee. Each of these assignments could be considered a typical female committee appointment.

Women were placed with somewhat lesser frequency on other committees that were deemed appropriate for their gender. Two women were assigned to Public Safety, School and Public Lands, and Enrolled and Engrossed Bills, a "housekeeping" committee.

Nellie Olson of Wilton was the first woman to serve on the important Judiciary Committee. She served a single term in 1937. Credit: State Historical Society of North Dakota

Few women who served during this twenty-four year period were awarded seats on traditionally male standing committees. Minnie Craig was the only woman who served on Ways and Means, Appropriations, or Banking. This last committee was an obvious choice for Craig, who was a banker. The lone woman to serve on either Agriculture or two agriculture-related committees (Livestock and Drainage and Irrigation) was Brynhild Haugland, a farmer. Nellie Olson, who served a single term in 1937, was the only woman assigned to Judiciary. Two women were appointed to Election and Election Privileges, a committee which would be subsumed by Judiciary in 1947. Rules, Joint Rules, Joint Committee on Rural Institutions, Public Debt, Joint Committee on Labor, and Joint Insurance each had only one female member.

The above discussion is illustrated graphically in table 1 which indicates that over 70 percent of female committee assignments between 1923 and 1946 were to committees that dealt with traditionally female concerns. Only 29 percent were to nontraditional or "male" committees.

Table 1.—Committee assignments, 1923-1946

Periods & (total No. of assignments)	No. & (%) to trad. female	No. & (%) to trad. male
1923-1946 (52)	37 (71)	15 (29)
1947-1969 ___	_____	_____
1970-1979 ___	_____	_____
1980-1989 ___	_____	_____

Ten women began their service in the legislature between 1947 when the standing committees were reorganized and 1969. Brynhild Haugland, whose service continued, brought the number of women who served during this twenty-two year period to eleven.

Between 1947 and 1969 women continued to be assigned frequently to committees that dealt with education, health, and welfare. Eight (73 percent) of the eleven women were assigned to Education. Six (55 percent) were assigned to Social Welfare, a committee that incorporated Public Welfare, Public Health, Public Safety, and Temperance. Fewer women (only three or 27 percent) were seated on Political Subdivisions, a committee devoted to yet another traditional female interest—local government.

After legislative reorganization in 1947 women continued to be less frequently assigned to most of the traditionally male committees. Only one woman, Sybil Kelly, served on Appropriations. Rosamund O'Brien was the lone woman on Natural Resources and likewise Fern Lee on Transportation. When someone suggested that Transportation was an

Brynhild Haugland, a Ward County farmer, was assigned to the Agriculture Committee in 1939, her first session in the House. She was the first woman on the committee and one of only two women seated on the committee before 1970. Credit: State Historical Society of North Dakota.

unlikely committee choice for a woman, Lee "defended her viewpoint saying, 'Safety laws and such things are of direct interest to women.' "[88] Sybil Kelly and Brynhild Haugland were the only women to serve on Agriculture. Nettie Ellingson, who was in insurance, and Rosamund O'Brien, who was in publishing, were assigned to Industry and Business. O'Brien and Grace Stone sat on Finance and Taxation.

While women's representation on a majority of the traditionally male committees was low, more frequent assignments to several "male" committees pointed to a shift in the established pattern of female committee assignments. Three women were placed on General Affairs and Labor Relations. Four women were assigned to State and Federal Government, the first assignment going to Brynhild Haugland in 1949. There was a sharp rise in the number of women who were assigned to Judiciary, traditionally a man's committee. While only one woman served on this committee before 1947, eight received appointment to Judiciary between 1947 and 1969. Education ranked with Judiciary as a committee for women.

Table 2 indicates that only 29 percent of women legislators' committee assignments between 1923 and 1946 were to committees devoted to traditionally male concerns. In the succeeding period, the percentage of these assignments increased to 54 percent. This shift in the pattern of women's committee assignments indicates that by the Fifties and Sixties North Dakota's women legislators were frequently addressing nontraditional policy domains.

Table 2.—Committee assignments, 1923-1969

Periods & (total No. of assignments)	No. & (%) to trad. female	No. & (%) to trad. male
1923-1946 (52)	37 (71)	15 (29)
1947-1969 (35)	16 (46)	19 (54)
1970-1979 ___	_____	_____
1980-1989 ___	_____	_____

Committee Chairs and Other Leadership Positions

A common theme in studies of women lawmakers on the state and national level is the underrepresentation of women in positions of leadership on committees, particularly "important" committees, and in House and Senate chambers as a whole. In all the state legislatures represented in *Political Woman*, Jeane Kirkpatrick reported "a male monopoly of top leadership positions."[89] In her 1977 study of sex roles in state legislatures, Irene Diamond observed that "important leadership positions are more commonly held by the men."[90] By the mid-1980s women legislators comprised nearly 15 percent of state legislative seats in the United States, while holding about 9.5 percent of all committee chairs and about 10.5 percent of other leadership positions, such as majority and minority leaders.[91] In his 1984 study of the first one hundred U.S. congresswomen, Irwin Gertzog noted that few women have chaired House standing committees and no woman has ever served in a top leadership position in the House.[92]

In North Dakota committee chairs as well as committee vice chairs are almost always members of the majority party. Leadership positions on committees are selected in a manner similar to committee assignments. The Speaker of the House chooses committee leaders after consulting with the majority leader. In the Senate the committee on committees has this responsibility.[93]

Between 1923 and 1969 four of North Dakota's women legislators chaired standing committees, two in the House and two in the Senate. Three of the four women were Republican. Republican female committee chairs outnumbered Democratic female committee chairs because the Republicans dominated the legislature throughout most of the period.

The first woman to head a standing committee was Minnie Craig, appointed chair of the Banks and Banking Committee during her second session in the House. A banker by occupation, Craig was a staunch supporter of the Bank of North Dakota who, from early in her legislative career, spoke out on banking issues.[94]

In 1925, the session in which she served as chair of Banking, Craig asked to head the Appropriations Committee but was denied in favor of Frank Vogel. Apparently to compensate her for the denial, Speaker of the House B. C. Larkin promised Craig an appointment to the state Budget Board that fall. Because that appointment normally went to the chair of Appropriations, Larkin extracted a promise from Vogel that he would resign as chair of Appropriations in time to make way for Craig's appointment to that board. When the time came, a reluctant Vogel did resign and the governor appointed Craig to the Budget Board. Although Craig never chaired the Appropriations Committee, she felt that the honor was divided between her and Vogel in the 1925 session.[95] Had Craig not been elected Speaker of the House in 1933, she would have been appointed chair of Appropriations, a committee on which she was considered nearly irreplaceable.[96]

Brynhild Haugland was the second woman to chair a standing committee, Public Welfare. First appointed chair in 1941, Haugland headed the House's social welfare committee for a total of twenty-three sessions. In at least one session, Haugland herself carried every bill dealing with social welfare onto the floor.[97]

In 1951 Agnes Geelan chaired Labor Relations in the Senate, and in 1955 Rosamund O'Brien chaired Social Welfare. O'Brien also chaired a procedural committee, Enrolled and Engrossed Bills, for two sessions.

Two women, both Democrats, served in secondary leadership capacities on committees during this period. After

Appointed vice-chair of the House Social Welfare Committee in 1965, Anna Powers of Leonard was one of a handful of women who held a legislative leadership position before 1970. Credit: State Historical Society of North Dakota

chairing Social Welfare in the Senate in 1955, Rosamund O'Brien served as vice-chair in 1957. In 1965 Anna Powers of Leonard was appointed vice-chair of the Social Welfare Committee in the House. Powers went on to serve as vice-chair of State and Federal Government in the 1970s.

In addition to committee chairs, each legislative chamber has a presiding officer. The Speaker of the House presides over the House and in the Senate the lieutenant governor presides and is called President of the Senate. The Senate elects a president pro tempore to serve in the absence of the President of the Senate. The president pro tem is always a member of the majority party.[98] Each chamber also has a majority leader and a minority leader, an assistant majority leader and an assistant minority leader (also called "whips"), and a caucus leader for each party.

Minnie Craig was the only woman to serve in a top leadership position during the period 1923 to 1969. Craig's rise to leadership as Speaker of the House in 1933 was unprecedented in North Dakota and the nation. The significance of her appointment was not lost on her fellow House members. In placing Craig's name in nomination, H.F. Sweet declared:

"We are making history today. . . . The candidate that I am about to mention is a woman. I believe, Mr. Chief Clerk, that never before in the history of this state, or so far as I know in the history of the United States—and very likely the history of the world—never before has a woman been accorded the honor of presiding over a legislative session."[99]

The evening before the election of Speaker of the House, Nonpartisan League legislators, who controlled the House in 1933, had selected Craig as their candidate for the position.[100] The League's selection of a woman for the speakership was thought "not such a radical step for them as it might appear, for they have a tradition of fairness to women."[101] Apparently Craig's selection was not simply the result of the good graces of her fellow Nonpartisan League legislators. According to newspaper reports, Craig sought the position of Speaker and "did some clever political maneuvering to get the necessary indorsement [sic]."[102] The morning following her endorsement by the League Minnie Craig was elected Speaker of the House by a unanimous vote.[103]

The press was keenly interested in the first female Speaker of the House. Craig received requests for her photograph from newspapers in this country and in Europe,[104] and articles about her appeared in newspapers such as the *Boston Sunday Globe*, the *Christian Science Monitor*, and the *New York Times*.[105] Articles noted this veteran legislator's impressive record in past sessions and the fact that she had the

The press made much of the domestic prowess of Minnie Craig, as illustrated in this photograph taken at their request. Credit: North Dakota Institute for Regional Studies

support of her House colleagues, one of whom was quoted as saying:

> "We can trust her. We know her to be absolutely honest, broad in vision and tolerant of other people's rights, sympathetic to needed reform and untiring in effort to achieve it. We are mindful of the fact that through her legislative experience and her happy disposition, through her voice and seasoned judgement, she has the attributes that go to make a successful speaker. We have chosen quality."[106]

This 1933 editorial cartoon depicted Speaker of the House Minnie Craig as a slender, rolling pin wielding teacher. Credit: North Dakota Institute for Regional Studies

The press also commented extensively on her domestic qualities and physical appearance. A photograph of Craig doing the dishes (a photograph which, according to Craig, was taken at the press's request)[107] appeared in several east coast newspapers.[108] The *Monitor* described Craig as a woman who "can wield a gavel as well as she can wipe a dish."[109] The *New York Herald Tribune* noted that the first woman to preside in two houses "does her own housework."[110]

The press also reported on her considerable musical ability, her love of gardening, and her reputation as "a capable homemaker, an excellent cook, a fine needlewoman and a pleasing hostess."[111] Physical descriptions of Craig seldom failed to mention her lower jaw, which was said to be "firm"[112] and "determined." According to the press, Craig dressed neatly, "generally in dark colors and simple modes" and that she had black bobbed hair and wore glasses.[113]

After some puzzlement, the question of how to address the House's female presiding officer was resolved and Craig was referred to as "Madame Speaker."[114] According to the press, the leadership style of "Madame Speaker" was that of a school mistress and the atmosphere in the House in 1933 was that of a classroom.[115] An editorial in the *Ray Pioneer* expressed sympathy for Craig for having "to hold that bunch of unruly 'school boys' in line." The editorial was accompanied by a cartoon picturing a slim Craig dressed in a sheath standing behind a desk and wielding a rolling pin. Her chin is more pointed than determined.[116] The message of this image is that in this particular era of women's participation in politics a female leader had to be seen in terms of "teacher" and "homemaker," two roles for women with which society was comfortable and familiar.

Minnie Craig revealed in her unpublished autobiography the frustrations and disappointments she experienced as Speaker of the House in 1933. A constant source of annoyance was Chief Clerk James Curran's habit of signing his name to engrossed bills where Craig's signature was supposed to go. Perhaps even more frustrating to Craig was that she was never consulted or informed about procedural strategy. She felt that she was treated like an outsider by male legislators whom she described as "so accustomed to 'running things,' they didn't want my point of view."[117] Craig had come up against what others would refer to as the "old boys' club" or the "old boy network."

The lack of assistance from the Nonpartisan League floor leader frustrated Craig. He was rarely in his seat and frequently absent from the chamber. The changing of their votes after some legislators observed the way Craig voted aggravated the Speaker. In 1933 the House met in temporary, inadequate quarters in the Bismarck Municipal Auditorium because the capitol had burned in late 1930, compounding Craig's difficulties.[118]

Minnie Craig announced in June 1933 that she would not seek reelection to the legislature. A broken ankle and her new job as field worker for the Federal Emergency Relief Administration were presumably reasons for her retirement. In announcing her retirement, Craig expressed her appreciation for the cooperation and support that she had received from men and women during her time in office. She added, however, the following observation:

"After all, men don't like to follow a woman. They may appreciate her services, but they are much happier when those services are confined to a secretarial job, to routine work."[119]

In assessing Craig's role as Speaker of the House, political historian Larry Remele wrote:

"Mrs. Craig persevered despite exclusion from strategy meetings of her own faction; her ability to overcome the obstacles contributed much to the success of the session, one which convened at the depths of the worst agricultural

56

depression in state history and one which considered much remedial legislation of long lasting impact."[120]

Twenty years passed before another woman was elected as a speaker of the house in the United States. In 1953 Consuelo Northrup Bailey became Speaker of the Vermont House of Representatives.[121] Fifty years passed before another woman would become Speaker of the House in North Dakota. In 1983 Patricia "Tish" Kelly became the second woman to serve as Speaker of the North Dakota House of Representatives.[122]

Sponsored Legislation

One of the major roles of a legislator is sponsoring legislation in the form of bills and resolutions. Sponsored legislation is a reliable indicator of a lawmaker's legislative priorities.[123] These priorities, whether enacted or not, have an impact on the legislature as an institution by broadening views of what are legitimate issues for a legislative body to consider.[124]

Given the importance of legislative priorities to the legislative process, the following questions relative to the priorities of North Dakota's women legislators need to be raised. To what extent have North Dakota's women legislators sponsored legislation that deals with issues deemed to be peculiarly within the interest of their gender? To what extent have they expanded the scope of their legislation into policy areas not traditionally thought of as women's concern? And finally, have North Dakota's women legislators brought to the legislative agenda particular issues that affect women as a class by way of their sponsored legislation? If, as studies have concluded, "one type of power is bringing issues to the agenda that have been suppressed or overlooked,"[125] the extent to which North Dakota's women legislators have introduced these issues is a measure of their impact on the institution.

A key to answering these questions lies in an analysis of bill and resolution sponsorships by women during the thirty-five sessions that this study encompasses. Recognizing that overlapping occurs, bills and resolutions are classified into one of three categories: (1) those that address traditionally female issues, specifically, health, education, welfare, and children; (2) those that address nontraditional issues, such as "manufacturing and trade, business and finance, agriculture, taxation, public works (and other matters that encourage horse trading for palpably parochial benefits), civil, criminal and constitutional law, and the appropriations process;"[126] and (3) those that address issues directly affecting women as a class in their roles as mothers, wives, and homemakers and in their positions in the workplace, in government, and in education.[127]

Women who served in the legislature between 1923 and 1969 were involved 576 times in sponsoring legislation.[128] The actual number of bills and resolutions is less than this figure because two or more women co-sponsored some legislation. Four hundred eight (70 percent) of these legislative sponsorships involved traditionally male issues. Legislation in this category included taxes, insurance, elections, weather modification, zoning, corrections, libraries, wages, labor relations, water projects, banking, fairs, and legislative procedures. Appropriation legislation often called for funding for construction, maintenance, and repair of public buildings. Legislation dealing with agriculture and agricultural products and public safety were commonly sponsored or cosponsored. Numerous pieces of legislation sought to regulate and license a wide variety of professions from chauffeurs and watchmakers to nurses and hairdressers.

One hundred forty-eight (25 percent) of the women's legislative sponsorships involved issues of traditional interest—health, welfare, education, and children. Again, this legislation covered a wide range of subject matter.

Disease control and treatment, development and enhancement of medical programs and facilities, and extension of health services to rural North Dakotans were some of the health priorities. Alcohol abuse first received attention when in 1923 Nellie Dougherty sponsored a bill that made it a misdemeanor to operate a motor vehicle while intoxicated and provided for a penalty.

Welfare-related legislation provided for a wide range of public assistance programs, including aid to the blind, the poor, the elderly, and the disabled. Development and enhancement of special care facilities and the creation and governance of welfare agencies were addressed numerous times. Women legislators' consistent and intensive activity on the public welfare committee is evident in the level and depth of their legislative sponsorships in this area. For example, for over fifty years Brynhild Haugland had a part in writing the enabling legislation necessary to receive and implement all federally-funded public assistance programs in North Dakota.[129]

Legislative sponsorships in the area of education dealt with, among other things, school buildings and lands, teacher contracts and certification, curriculum, special needs students, tuition, and school district reorganization. Child-related legislation commonly addressed such issues as adoption, foster care, child abuse, juvenile court, day care, runaways, and contributing to the delinquency of minors.

Eighteen (3 percent) of the legislative sponsorships between 1923 and 1969 related to issues that affect women as a class in their roles as mothers, wives, and homemakers and in their positions in the workplace, in government, and in education. The actual number of bills introduced in this category was eleven.

Minnie Craig was the first woman to introduce legislation in this category. In 1927 she sponsored a bill providing that married women could act as administrators and executors of estates and as guardians of children. In rising to explain her vote on this measure, Craig said:

"In behalf of the married women of North Dakota, I feel it is my duty to thank the men of this House for their support of this measure. By their support and the passage of this measure, they will have assisted in bringing married women from 'civil death' in the eyes of the law to 'civil life.' I vote 'aye.' "[130]

In 1937 Nellie Olson sponsored two bills which specifically centered on the status of women: a bill to increase the dollar amount of mothers' pensions and a bill to provide for the selection of precinct committeewomen. In the 1941 session Brynhild Haugland sponsored a bill that provided for the selection of precinct, county, and state committeewomen.

During the 1950s Haugland sponsored three women-related bills. Two provided aid to mothers, in one case mothers with dependent children and in the other case unmarried mothers. The other expanded the residency rights of married women.

In the 1960s the interests of women in the workplace became important for the first time. In 1963 Anna Powers and Sybil Kelly co-sponsored a bill that called for equal pay for males and females for equal work. That same year Congress passed the federal Equal Pay Act. Until this time employers could pay women less than men for the same work without consequence.[131] During the 1963 session Anna Powers sponsored a bill related to minimum wages and hours for working women. In 1965 Powers sponsored an equal pay bill which included the concept of comparable worth. In 1967 five women sponsored legislation that equalized women's rights and responsibilities to serve on juries.

The last and most controversial bill dealt with abortion. Sponsored in 1969 by Aloha Eagles, it provided for the liberalization of North Dakota's abortion law, which at the time permitted abortion only to save the life of the mother. Eagles was threatened for this sponsorship and the police provided her with protection for a period of time during the session.[132] Eagles lists her work on "women's legislation," including abortion rights, the Equal Rights Amendment, rape, and abuse, as her major accomplishment as a legislator.[133]

Summary and Conclusion

From the foregoing discussion of the twenty women who served in the North Dakota legislature between 1923 and 1969, this brief collective profile emerges. North Dakota's first twenty female legislators tended to be married, to have no active child-rearing responsibilities, and to be in their late forties when first elected to the legislature. They were well educated for women of the time and frequently combined homemaking with employment outside the home. Employment outside the home tended to be in an occupation not ordinarily considered a "feminine" occupation, most notably farming, business, journalism or sales. The majority were from the eastern half of the state, were aligned with one of two factions of the Republican party, and were single-term legislators.

Not an ethnically diverse group, North Dakota's first women legislators were more often than not of Scandinavian or British Isles ancestry. They were predominantly Protestants, with Lutherans outnumbering all other Protestant denominations.

Nearly half of the first twenty women in the legislature held an elective office before becoming legislators. All but one of these women served on a county or city school board or as county superintendent of schools. A majority were active in precinct, district, or state political party organizations before their legislative election and nearly half claimed

61

family roots in electoral politics. They were members of partisan and nonpartisan political organizations as well as a wide range of other organizations.

Although North Dakota's first twenty female legislators held a variety of legislative interests, the interest they most commonly shared was education. Interest in public welfare and particularly the welfare of women, children, and the elderly was also common. These interests were reflected in their committee assignments, with women being well represented on Education and Social Welfare. Women legislators were infrequently assigned to traditionally male standing committees. After legislative reorganization in 1947, more female assignments were made to traditionally male committees than in the earlier part of the period, with the most significant increase in the number of women who served on Judiciary.

Four of the first twenty women to serve in the North Dakota legislature chaired standing committees. Two chaired committees traditionally considered "male" committees (Banking and Labor Relations) and two chaired a committee traditionally associated with women's concerns (Social Welfare). The lone woman to serve in a major leadership position was Minnie Craig, who was elected Speaker of the House in 1933.

North Dakota's first twenty female legislators were involved 576 times in sponsoring bills and resolutions between 1923 and 1969. Seventy-one percent of these legislative sponsorships addressed nontraditional issues, while 26 percent addressed traditional. Only 3 percent addressed issues that affected women as a class. Few as they were, they represented the earliest attempts of North Dakota's women legislators to bring to the legislative agenda particularly, if not uniquely, female issues.

This collective profile provides a base from which to explore the backgrounds and legislative careers of the women who entered the legislature in the 1970s and 1980s. Though few in number, North Dakota's pioneer women lawmakers forged a place for themselves and later women in the world of legislative politics. Through their committee assignments and legislative sponsorships, they addressed and advanced a wide range of issues in both traditional and nontraditional domains. By the end of the period they had initiated nearly a dozen pieces of legislation addressing issues that affected women as a class.

Among their ranks were Minnie Craig, Brynhild Haugland, Agnes Geelan, and Rosamund O'Brien, who proved that women could secure and handle top legislative leadership positions. Craig, who reached the highest ranks of the legislative hierarchy only to find male colleagues unwilling to follow her direction, paved the way for future female leaders such as Agnes Geelan, who stated, "I didn't have to prove myself because of Minnie Craig."[134] Each of the twenty women who served in the North Dakota legislature between 1923 and 1969 made her mark by affirming with her very presence Eleanor Roosevelt's declaration that in the male world of politics, "Women are Here to Stay."[135]

Chapter 1 End Notes

[1]Eleanor Roosevelt and Lorena A. Hickok, *Ladies of Courage* (New York: G. P. Putnam's Sons, 1954), 290.

[2]Minnie D. Craig, handwritten autobiography, Minnie D. Craig Papers, North Dakota Institute for Regional Studies, North Dakota State University, Fargo, 70-71.

[3]Carl Hennemann, "Politics No Pink Tea, Woman Solon Says," source unavailable, [1950], Brynhild Haugland Newspaper Clippings Collection, privately held, Minot.

[4]Paula Baker, "The Domestication of Politics: Women and American Political Society, 1780-1920," *American Historical Review* 89 (June 1984): 620-47.

[5]Bill G. Reid, "Elizabeth Preston Anderson and the Politics of Reform," in *The North Dakota Political Tradition*, ed. Thomas Howard, North Dakota Centennial Heritage Series, vol. 1 (Ames: Iowa State University Press, 1981), 189.

[6]Ibid., 195-97.

[7]Martin Gruberg, *Women in American Politics: An Assessment and Sourcebook* (Oshkosh: Academia Press, 1968), 220.

[8]Marcella Andre, "They Won the Right to Vote...But Little More," *Red River Valley Historian* (Summer 1975): 9.

[9]Ibid., 14.

[10]Ibid., 12-13.

[11]Ibid., 14.

[12]North Dakota Tax Department, "Women Successful in Statewide General Elections," 16 February 1988.

[13]William H. Chafe, *The American Woman: Her Changing Social, Economic, and Political Roles, 1920-1970* (New York: Oxford University Press, 1972), 22-28.

[14]Susan M. Hartmann, *From Margin to Mainstream: American Women and Politics Since 1960* (New York: Alfred A. Knopf, Inc., 1989), 1-21.

[15]Women were and still are thinly scattered in state senates across the country and in the United States Senate. According to Irene Diamond in her 1977 publication *Sex Roles in the State House*, the status of senates as "upper" houses is the reason for the sparse representation of women in these chambers. See Irene Diamond, Sex Roles in the State House (New Haven: Yale University Press, 1977), 9.

[16]Lynn Severson, "Women and North Dakota Politics," in *Day In, Day Out: Women's Lives in North Dakota*, ed. Bjorn Benson, Elizabeth

Hampsten, and Kathryn Sweney (Grand Forks: University of North Dakota, 1988), 205.

[17]Joe Ruff, "Minot's Haugland is U.S.'s longest-serving legislator," *Grand Forks Herald*, 19 March 1987.

[18]"Long Term Lady Legislator Has Heart for the Farm," *Bismarck Tribune*, 2 March 1951.

[19]Elwyn Robinson, *History of North Dakota* (Lincoln: University of Nebraska Press, 1966), 353-54, 371-79.

[20]Larry Remele, "North Dakota History: Overview and Summary," in *North Dakota Centennial Blue Book, 1889-1989*, ed. Curtis Ericksmoen (Bismarck: Secretary of State, 1989), 37.

[21]Robinson, 388-95.

[22]Remele, 38-39.

[23]Irwin N. Gertzog, *Congressional Women: Their Recruitment, Treatment, and Behavior* (New York: Praeger Publishers, 1984), 35.

[24]"North Dakota's First Woman Solons Mum On Tactics They Will Use," *Fargo Forum*, [January 1923], Minnie Craig Scrapbook.

[25]"Two Women Members of State Assembly," *Fargo Forum*, [January 1923], Minnie Craig Scrapbook.

[26]John Andrews, "Between the Acts," *Fargo Courier-News*, [January 1923], Minnie Craig Scrapbook.

[27]Ruth B. Mandel, "The Political Woman," in *The American Woman, 1988-89: A Status Report*, ed. Sara E. Rix (New York: W.W. Norton and Company, 1988), 96.

[28]Jeane J. Kirkpatrick, *Political Woman* (New York: Basic Books, 1974), 55.

[29]Mary Carolyn Ellis and Joanne V. Hawks, "Creating a Different Pattern: Florida's Women Legislators, 1928-1986," *Florida Historical Quarterly* 65 (July 1987): 76. For other studies of women legislators in southern states by these authors, see Joanne V. Hawks, M. Carolyn Ellis, and J. Byron Morris, "Women in the Mississippi Legislature (1924-1981)," *Journal of Mississippi History* 43, no. 4 (November 1981): 266-93; Joanne Varner Hawks, "A Select Few: Alabama's Women Legislators, 1922-1983," *Alabama Review* 38 (1985): 175-201; M. Carolyn Ellis and Joanne V. Hawks, "Ladies in the Gentlemen's Club: South Carolina Women Legislators, 1928-1984," in *The Proceedings of the South Carolina Historical Association*, ed. William S. Brockinton (Aiken: South Carolina Historical Association, 1986), 17-32; Joanne V. Hawks and Mary Carolyn Ellis, "Heirs of the Southern Progressive Tradition: Women in Southern Legislatures in the 1920s," in *Southern Women*, ed. Caroline Matheny Dillman (New York: Hemisphere Publishing Company, 1988), 81-92; Joanne V. Hawks and Mary Carolyn Ellis, "Women Legislators in the Lower South: South Carolina,

Georgia, Alabama, and Mississippi, 1822-1984," in *Women in the South: An Anthropological Perspective*, ed. Holly F. Mathews (Athens: University of Georgia Press, 1989), 110-121.

[30]"Getting Ready For Business At Bismarck," *Benson County Press*, [January 1923], Minnie Craig Scrapbook.

[31]Marilyn Johnson and Kathy Stanwick, *Profile of Women Holding Office* (New Brunswick, NJ: Center for the American Woman and Politics, Eagleton Institute of Politics, Rutgers University, 1976), xxx.

[32]Bernice T. Van Der Vries, "Women in Government," *State Government* (June 1948): 128.

[33]R. R. Morgan, "Death Takes Harry O'Brien, Press Editor," *Walsh County Press*, 15 October 1953, 1.

[34]North Dakota Legislative Council, *Journal of the Senate of the Thirty-third Session of the Legislative Assembly*, 351.

[35]"Death Takes Harry O'Brien."

[36]Kirkpatrick, 230.

[37]"TRUST IN SELF, SAYS SPEAKER."

[38]Marcia Harris, "Life of Hard Political Work Shows Rewards," *Bismarck Tribune*, 21 November 1982.

[39]"The First Mother of Our District in the Legislature," *Williams County Farmers Press*, 9 January 1929, 3.

[40]Vera Gothberg, telephone interview by author, 24 March 1990.

[41]Agnes "Peggy" Linha, "Women Legislators History Project Survey," completed 18 October 1989. Held by author.

[42]Audrey Gruger, telephone interview by author, 24 March 1990.

[43]Opal Hultberg, telephone interview by author, 20 October, 1989.

[44]Betty Kummer, telephone interview by author, 25 March 1990.

[45]Johnson and Stanwick, xxxvii.

[46]Gertzog, 38-39, 45.

[47]Emmy E. Werner, "Women in the State Legislatures," *Western Political Quarterly* 21, no. 1 (March 1968): 45-46.

[48]Johnson and Stanwick, xxxviii.

[49]William Sherman, *Prairie Mosaic: An Ethnic Atlas of Rural North Dakota* (Fargo: North Dakota Institute for Regional Studies, 1983), 1.

[50]William Sherman, preface to *Plains Folk: North Dakota's Ethnic History*, edited by William Sherman and Playford Thorson, North Dakota Centennial Heritage Series, vol. 2 (Fargo: North Dakota Institute for Regional Studies, 1988), 1.

[51]Robert P. Wilkins, "People of the British Isles," in *Plains Folk: North Dakota's Ethnic History*, ed. William Sherman and Playford Thorson, North Dakota Centennial Heritage Series, vol. 2 (Fargo: North Dakota Institute for Regional Studies, 1988), 54.

[52]Sherman, Prairie Mosaic, 3.

[53]Playford Thorson, "Scandinavians," in *Plains Folk: North Dakota's Ethnic History,* ed. William Sherman and Playford Thorson, North Dakota Centennial Heritage Series, vol. 2 (Fargo: North Dakota Institute for Regional Studies, 1988), 194.

[54]Ibid., 185.

[55]Gertzog, 6, 36-37.

[56]Ibid., 39-41.

[57]Werner, 46.

[58]Johnson and Stanwick, xl-xli.

[59]"North Dakota's Women Legislators," *Bismarck Tribune*, 3 March 1929, Minnie Craig Scrapbook.

[60]Karen Starr, "Fighting for a Future: Farm Women of the Nonpartisan League," *Minnesota History* (Summer 1983): 256.

[61]"North Dakota's First Woman Solons."

[62]"North Dakota's Woman Legislators."

[63]Pearl Andre, ed. and comp., *Women on the Move* (Bismarck: *Bismarck Tribune*, 1975), 116.

[64]Lou Hiller, "Mrs. Milton Kelly State Representative, Follows Father's Steps-50 Years Later," *Bismarck Tribune*, 6 February 1959, 5.

[65]Johnson and Stanwick, xxxiv.

[66]Ellis and Hawks, "Creating a Different Pattern," 73.

[67]Hartmann, 15-17.

[68]Paul Windels, "Garbage dispute spurred formation of Fargo League," Fargo Forum, 10 July 1988.

[69]"A False Alarm," *Williams County Farmers Press*, 20 November 1929, 2.

[70]Kirkpatrick, 152-53; Diamond, 89-90.

[71]"Recommendations and Reactions: Report of the Second Arizona Women's Town Hall on the Subject of Women and the Arizona Political Process," in *Women and the Arizona Political Process*, ed. Rita Mae Kelly (Lanham, MD: University Press of America, 1988), 137. For information about women legislators in other states, see Leon Anderson, *New Hampshire Women Legislators: 1921-1971* (Concord, NH: New Hampshire Savings

Bank, 1971); Carol Blake, comp., "Women in the Pennsylvania Legislature, 1922-1982" (n.p.: Legislative Reference Bureau, 1983); Janet Boles, "The Texas Women in Politics," *Social Science Journal* 21, no. 1 (January 1984): 79-89; Mary Brown, *Women in the Legislative Process* (Lansing: Michigan House of Representatives, 1984); Louise Holland Coe, *Lady and the Law Books: Sixteen Years First and Only Woman Member of the New Mexico Senate* (Albuquerque: By the author, 1981); Barbara Gooding, *Women in the Washington State Legislature, 1913-1983* (Olympia, WA: By the author, 1983); Anna Mae Goss, "Illinois Women in Congress and the General Assembly," *Research Response* (April 1989): 1-14; Louise Johnson, *Women of the Louisiana Legislature* (Farmerville, LA: Greenbay Publishing, 1986); Susan Gluck Mezey, "Women and Representation: The Case of Hawaii," *Journal of Politics* 40, no. 2 (May 1978): 369-85; Jacqueline P. Payne, comp., Women of the Mississippi Legislature (Jackson: Mississippi Library Commission, 1980); and Jean Bickmore White, "Gentle Persuaders: Utah's First Women Legislators," *Utah Historical Quarterly* 38, no. 1 (1970): 31-49.

[72]Hiller.

[73]"Women Members of Legislature Both Have Teaching Experience," *Bismarck Tribune*, [January 1923], Minnie Craig Scrapbook.

[74]Aloha Eagles, "Women Legislators History Project Survey," completed 18 May 1989. Held by author.

[75]"North Dakota's Women Legislators."

[76]Kirkpatrick, 125-26.

[77]Lloyd Omdahl, *1989-91 Governing North Dakota and The Constitution of North Dakota* (Grand Forks: Bureau of Governmental Affairs, University of North Dakota, 1989), 59.

[78]Kirkpatrick, 125.

[79]Rita Mae Kelly, Jayne Burgess, and Katie Kaufmanis, "Arizona Women and the Legislature," in *Women and the Arizona Political Process*, Second Arizona Women's Town Hall, Soroptimist International of Phoenix (Lanham, MD: University Press of America, 1988), 45.

[80]Gertzog, 129-39.

[81]Kirkpatrick, 125-126.

[82]Ibid.

[83]Robinson, 433.

[84]North Dakota Legislative Council, *Senate and House Rules and Committees*, 1947, 29-30.

[85]Gen Middaugh, "Rep. Haugland Finishing 15th Term," *Bismarck Tribune*, 2 March 1967.

[86]North Dakota Legislative Council, *Senate and House Rules and Committees, 1971*, 41-43.

[87]Craig autobiography, 29-30.

[88]Dorothy Hager, "One Veteran and Four Novices Proving It Isn't All Man's World In Legislature Session," *Minot Daily News*, 31 January 1967.

[89]Kirkpatrick, 222.

[90]Diamond, 46.

[91]Nadine Brozan, "State Legislature: Center Stage for Women," *New York Times*, 18 November 1985, in *Report from a Conference: Women in Legislative Leadership*, by the Center for the American Woman and Politics (New Brunswick, NJ: Center for the American Woman and Politics, Eagleton Institute of Politics, Rutgers University, [1986]), 57.

[92]Gertzog, 93, 139.

[93]Omdahl, 62.

[94]"Benson County Legislator Boosts Bank of North Dakota," *Nonpartisan Leader*, [December 1922], Minnie Craig Scrapbook.

[95]Craig autobiography, 30-49.

[96]"Legislators Face Leadership Joust," in *Bismarck Tribune*, 31 December 1932, Minnie Craig Scrapbook.

[97]Jill Schramm, "'The Dean' marks 50 years," *Minot Daily News*, 22 March 1987, 1.

[98]Omdahl, 58-9.

[99]North Dakota Legislative Council, Rep. H. F. Sweet Comments on House floor, 3 January 1933, *Journal of the House of the Twenty-third Session of the Legislative Assembly*, 5.

[100]"Woman Legislator Selected by Party for Important Job," *Bismarck Tribune*, 3 January 1933. Minnie Craig Scrapbook.

[101]"Woman's Sagacity Wins Gavel of North Dakota Speakership: Nonpartisan League Honors Mrs. Minnie Craig for Ability," *Christian Science Monitor*, 16 January 1933. Minnie Craig Scrapbook.

[102]"Maine Woman as Speaker Rules North Dakota's Lower House," *Boston Sunday Globe*, 15 January 1933. Minnie Craig Scrapbook.

[103]"Woman Named Speaker of House in North Dakota Legislature: Mrs. Minnie D.Craig Becomes First to Serve in Nation," *Minneapolis Journal*, 3 January 1933. Minnie Craig Scrapbook.

[104]Craig autobiography, 54.

[105]Minnie Craig Scrapbook, 17-18.

[106]"Woman's Sagacity Wins Gavel."

[107]Minnie Craig Scrapbook, handwritten note, 22.

[108]Ibid., 17, 22, 32.

[109]"Woman's Sagacity Wins Gavel."

[110]"Woman Presides in 2 Houses, Her Own and North Dakota's," *New York Herald Tribune*, 8 January 1933. Minnie Craig Scrapbook.

[111]"Minnie Craig—First Woman House Speaker," source unavailable, 16 January 1933. Minnie Craig Scrapbook.

[112]" 'We Can Trust You': Nonpartisan League Recites Faith in Woman Speaker of House," *Washington Daily Report*, 5 January 1933. Minnie Craig Scrapbook.

[113]"Maine Woman as Speaker."

[114]"Minnie Craig Will Be Called Madame Speaker," *Grand Forks Herald*, 5 January 1933, 1.

[115]"TRUST IN SELF, SAYS SPEAKER."

[116]" 'Give It To 'em Minnie,' " *Ray Pioneer*, [January 1933]. Minnie Craig Scrapbook.

[117]Craig autobiography, 59-60.

[118]Ibid., 58, 60-61.

[119]"Minnie Craig No Candidate For Election," source unavailable, [June 1934]. Minnie Craig Scrapbook.

[120][Larry Remele], Minnie Craig Biography File, State Archives and Historical Research Library, State Historical Society of North Dakota, Bismarck.

[121]John Mason Potter, "First N.E. Woman to Head Law-Making Body: Vermont Lawyer Blazing Path for Her Sex Is Being Hailed as Governor Prospect," source unavailable, 25 January 1953. Minnie Craig Scrapbook.

[122]"Madame Speaker the 2nd," *Fargo Forum*, 12 December, 1982.

[123]Gertzog, 161.

[124]Sue Thomas, "The Impact of Women on State Legislative Policy," Paper presented to the Annual Meeting of the American Political Science Association, Atlanta, GA, 1-4 September 1989, 14.

[125]Ibid., 7.

[126]Gertzog, 129-30.

[127]The author acknowledges the contribution of Michelle A. Saint-Germain to the development of the categories outlined in this section. For a longitudinal analysis of bills proposed by legislators in the Arizona legislature, see Michelle A. Saint-Germain, "Does Their Difference Make A Difference? The Impact of Elected Women on Public Policy in Arizona," *Social Science Quarterly* 70, no. 4 (December 1989): 956-968.

[128]For the content analysis of female legislative proposals, a brief title or description of each bill and resolution sponsored by a woman legislator was obtained from records held by the North Dakota Legislative Council. Proposals introduced between 1923 and 1941 were located in House and Senate journals. Those introduced beginning with the 1943 session have been entered on data base and were made available in computer printout form.

[129]Brynhild Haugland, "Women Legislators History Project Survey," completed 18 May 1989. Held by author.

[130]North Dakota Legislative Council, Rep. Minnie Craig Comments on House floor, 3 February 1927, *Journal of the House of the Twentieth Session of the Legislative Assembly*, 465.

[131]Hartmann, 53.

[132]"Abusive Phone Call To Fargo Solon Has Capitol in Uproar," *Fargo Forum*, 11 February 1969.

[133]Eagles survey.

[134]"Life of Hard Political Work."

[135]Roosevelt and Hickok, 221.

2

The Emergence of "Political Woman": The 1970s

The most important finding of this study is that political woman exists.[1]

—Jeane J. Kirkpatrick, 1974

Since time immemorial, women have been drafted to fill low-paying jobs; consequently, it's surprising that there haven't been more women involved in North Dakota politics.... Oh, we have provided more than our share of workers in the field. Scores of women put their hands, feet, and minds to work to elect men to office, but rare are the times that women have reached that status. The year 1972 may mark a change in that situation. Thirty-two women ran for State office and twelve were elected to the Legislature. Considering that there are 153 legislators, twelve may not seem much of a breakthrough; but considering that in the past our maximum was five, breakthrough it is.[2]

—Aloha Eagles, 1973

73

Historical Background and Overview

The emergence of women as a political force in the 1970s was an integral and important part of a dramatic shift of women's place in American life. A key element of the changing pattern of women's participation in politics was the upsurge in the number of women seeking and winning elective office. As a result of the influence of the contemporary women's movement, the public increasingly accepted the idea of women in office, and women as a group came to see themselves as potential candidates and officeholders.[3] Many of the women who sought public office in the wake of modern

Sixteen of the nineteen women serving in the legislature in 1977 were House members. They were (first row, left to right) Corliss Mushik, Ruth Meiers, Jean Herman, Burness Reed, Sister Mary Beauclair (second row, left to right) Tish Kelly, Pauline Benedict, Fern Lee, Aloha Eagles, (third row, left to right) Marjorie Kermott, Rosie Black, Brynhild Haugland, Anna Powers, (fourth row, left to right) Janet Wentz, Alice Olson, and Joann McCaffery (not pictured). Credit: Fred Schumacher

feminism attributed their growing political aspirations simply to individual decisions, not recognizing the role of the women's movement in raising public consciousness of women's right to such aspirations.[4]

During the Seventies women's total representation in federal, state, county, and local elective offices more than doubled. The number of women who served in state legislatures increased steadily during the decade. The total number of state women legislators in 1971 was three hundred and forty-four; by the 1979 sessions this number had risen to seven hundred and seventy. By the end of the decade women's overall representation in state legislatures had risen to above 10 percent.[5]

Even with this increase in the number of women officeholders during the 1970s, women remained vastly underrepresented in government bodies, including state legislatures. This fact led Jeane J. Kirkpatrick to conclude in her 1974 study of female legislators that "the most interesting question about women's political participation is why that role is so insignificant."[6] In a profile of women officeholders published by the Center for the American Woman and Politics two years later, authors Marilyn Johnson and Kathy Stanwick continued to ask, "Why are women absent from political roles?"[7]

As during the era 1923 through 1969, women's participation in the North Dakota legislature in the 1970s reflected dominant national trends. As the number of women in state legislatures nationwide steadily increased throughout the decade, so did the number of women in the North Dakota legislature. In the 1971 session five women were in the legislature. During the next three sessions women lawmakers increased in number from thirteen in 1973 to sixteen in 1975 to nineteen in 1977. By the 1979 session twenty women were counted among legislators. Women's representation in the legislature quadrupled during the period.

75

In the 1970s the total number of women who served in the North Dakota legislature was thirty-one. Five began their terms before 1970 and twenty-six commenced their legislative careers during the Seventies. The total number of female legislators during the prior five decades had been twenty.

The 1972 election saw the greatest single increase in the number of women whom the people elected to the legislature; twelve women won elections, more than doubling the number who gained seats in 1970. This unprecedented increase occurred the same year in which the U.S. Congress passed the Equal Rights Amendment, Congresswoman Shirley Chisholm of New York ran for the Democratic presidential nomination, and Republican Ann Armstrong became the first woman keynote speaker at a national convention of a major political party.[8]

The decade that brought a marked increase in women's representation in the legislature found North Dakota a modernized state continuing to deal with the boom-and-bust cycle in agriculture and other industries. The early 1970s saw record grain prices as well as high prices for land and machinery. This boom climate encouraged new and established farmers to expand their operations. By the end of the decade a decline in crop prices spelled a downswing for the rural economy. Energy industries boomed in the Seventies. As energy companies changed the face of western North Dakota, North Dakotans debated their impact and the state's treasury enjoyed increased extraction taxes from both the coal and oil industries.[9]

By the 1970s the Republican party's dominance of the state's political life had weakened. In 1960 the newly merged Democratic-NPL party succeeded in capturing the governorship, an office the party continued to hold throughout the Seventies.[10] From here on, members of the Democratic-NPL party will be referred to as Democrats. In 1965 House

76

Stella Fritzell of Grand Forks was elected chair of the legislative women's caucus when it was organized in 1975. Credit: State Historical Society of North Dakota

Democrats outnumbered House Republicans for the first time in the state's history. Control of the House, however, reverted to the Republicans in 1967. Though overall control of the legislature remained in the hands of the Republicans during the Seventies, the Democratic party increasingly challenged that control. In the 1977 session the numbers of Democrats equalled Republicans in the House. Republican control of the Senate remained steadfast.

In the 1970s women legislators' party loyalties continued to reflect the dominant political culture. Whereas 85 percent of the women who served in the legislature between 1923 and 1969 were aligned with the Republican party, in the 1970s sixteen (62 percent) of the twenty-six beginning women legislators were Republicans. Democratic women, on the other hand, increased their numbers from three in the previous period to ten in the Seventies; they now made up 38 percent of all first-term women legislators. All but one of the five whose service began before and continued into the Seventies were Republicans. Although Republican women legislators continued to outnumber their Democratic female colleagues, a shift in the pattern of party affiliation had occurred.

During the 1975 session Republican and Democratic women legislators formed a caucus, which according to the group's first chair, Stella Fritzell, was " 'a place where women can discuss their interests and become knowledgeable without being partisan.' "[11] Before 1975 female lawmakers had not met formally or informally as a group.[12] Caucus member Corliss Mushik recalled:

"When we first started it, we did call regular meetings about every two weeks. We met in the upper balcony early in the morning and the attendance was not large. But people did visit regularly and informal coalitions were formed where women would share in the proposals and bills that interested them most."[13]

According to Patricia "Tish" Kelly, who was a freshman legislator in 1975, the organization was "deliberately loose and unstructured, but it was a real serious effort to bring us together on issues we could agree on."[14] The legislative women's caucus continued to meet informally every session through 1989.[15]

While some patterns, such as party affiliation, saw change in the Seventies, others remained fairly stable. In keeping with tradition, women legislators remained concentrated in the House. Twenty-two (85 percent) of the twenty-six women who entered the legislature in the Seventies were elected to the House. Female House members had made up 90 percent of the women who served before 1970. All five of the women whose legislative careers began before and continued into the Seventies sat in the House of Representatives. Not a single female House member sought and won a seat in the "upper" chamber between 1970 and 1979.

Women from the eastern half of the state continued to outnumber women from the west. Sixteen (62 percent) of the twenty-six women who entered the legislature in the 1970s came from eastern counties (see figure 2). Before 1970 70 percent had come from eastern North Dakota. Three of the five women whose service extended into the Seventies were eastern North Dakotans. While no women from west of the Missouri River were elected to the legislature before 1970,

Fig. 2. Post offices of women entering the legislature in the 1970s. (Base map: North Dakota Highway Department.)

79

two women (Violetta LaGrave and Corliss Mushik) from west river country went to Bismarck in the 1970s.

Viewing geographical representation from another perspective reveals a pattern change. While six (30 percent) of the twenty women between 1923 and 1969 were elected from the cities of Grand Forks, Minot, and Fargo, sixteen (61 percent) of the twenty-six women who began their legislative tenures in the Seventies came from these cities and Bismarck. Of these sixteen women, seven (44 percent) were elected from Grand Forks. Fargo chose five of the sixteen.

The number of terms of service reveals another change in pattern. While eleven (55 percent) of the women before 1970 served only one term, only eight (31 percent) of the women first elected in the Seventies were one-term legislators. The largest increase was among those women who served between two and five terms, up over 17 percent. Those with six or more terms increased nearly 7 percent from the previous period. An increase in career-minded ventures into politics in the wake of the contemporary women's movement helps explain this change.[16]

Background Characteristics

The following discussion of background characteristics and legislative interests will focus on the twenty-six women who entered the legislature in the 1970s because the five women whose service began before and extended into the Seventies were discussed in the previous chapter. However, the focus will broaden in the sections on committee assignments, leadership positions, and sponsored legislation to include the five veteran legislators.

The influx of women who sought, won, and took legislative seats between late 1972 and early 1973 did not escape the attention of the press. After the November 1972 election, the *Grand Forks Herald* noted in an editorial that it was fifty years ago that month that Minnie Craig and Nellie

Dougherty had become the first two women elected to the state's legislature. The editorial reported with pride that more women would be in North Dakota's legislature the coming year than in any other state.[17]

The press, as it had in the 1920s, demonstrated considerable interest in the personal and professional backgrounds of the 1972 candidates. The *Fargo Forum*, for example, ran a lengthy article in October 1972 about the Fargo-area female legislative candidates. While the article provided a wide range of information about these candidates, there was extensive discussion of familial and personal considerations such as provisions for the care of children, husbands, households, and pets during campaigns and legislative sessions and appropriate attire for female candidates and officeholders. Readers came away knowing among other things which women were comfortable wearing pants and which women hired outside help to assist with house cleaning and/or child care.[18]

Once elected, the eleven women in the 1973 legislature, now recognized as "the largest group of women ever voted into the Legislature at one general election," continued to receive press attention. Given the personal nature of some of that attention, perhaps other newly-elected female legislators agreed with Violetta LaGrave of Mandan who stated, "Actually, I wish we weren't news."[19]

In a *Fargo Forum* article that appeared just before the 1974 election, female legislative candidates reported that they were better accepted in that campaign than in previous campaigns. Evidence of this, they believed, was a reduced interest in their families and what they wore and an increased interest in their stands on issues and their campaign strategies. Reflecting this shift in interest, the article that profiled these 1974 legislative candidates made no reference to the women's families, clothing or hair styles, but covered extensively their efforts at campaign financing.[20]

Age, Marital Status, and Number and Age of Children at Time of First Election to the Legislature

During the 1970s the median age of first-term women legislators saw little change from the previous period. While the median age of beginning women legislators was forty-eight between 1923 and 1969, the figure decreased only slightly, to forty-seven, during the Seventies.

As twenty-two year old Rosie Black of Grand Forks awaited the 1976 election results, she was soon to became the youngest woman elected to the legislature to date. Credit: Grand Forks Herald

Where the age pattern did change after 1970 was in the age range of first-term women legislators. While three-fourths of the women who entered the legislature before 1970 were in their forties and fifties when first elected, first-term women legislators in their forties and fifties constituted only slightly over half of all first-term women legislators in the Seventies. Increasing in number were women at both ends of the age spectrum. While no women in their twenties won election to the legislature before 1970, two such women began their legislative duty in the Seventies, Rosie Black and Terry Irving, both of Grand Forks. While only one woman in her sixties went to the legislature before 1970, four women in their sixties entered in the 1970s.

The 1970s, also, brought a change in the marital profile of novice female lawmakers. While the percentage of married first-term women legislators remained high (70 percent before 1970 and 69 percent during the Seventies), the percentage of single women decreased markedly (from 25 percent to 8 percent). The number of widows significantly increased from 5 percent to 19 percent. The 1970s brought the first divorced woman to the legislature.

Pauline Benedict of Berthold was the lone woman to enter the legislature by way of the "widow's route." Her succession to her husband's legislative seat was under slightly

Pauline Benedict, who served in the House in 1973 and 1975, was only the second woman to reach the legislature via the "widow's route." Credit: State Historical Society of North Dakota

different circumstances than those under which Rosamund O'Brien succeeded her husband, Harry O'Brien, in 1953. George W. Benedict had served the third district in the House during the 1973 and 1975 sessions and had planned to seek reelection in 1976 when he died unexpectedly on June 3, 1976. His widow, Pauline, who had campaigned with him and had accompanied him to Bismarck during his two sessions in the legislature, had no plans to run for his seat. However, because she had worked so closely with her husband, supporters saw Benedict as a logical candidate and encouraged her to make a bid. Because of the encouragement, Benedict did seek and ultimately won a House seat in the fall of 1976. Benedict, who saw her tenure in the House as a way of carrying on her husband's work, received assignments to the same committees on which her husband had served.[21]

While the percentage of first-term women legislators with no active child-rearing responsibilities remained high, the 1970s witnessed an increase in the percentage of beginning women lawmakers with one or more children under the age of eighteen. Before 1970 fifteen women legislators (75 percent of the total) either had no children or had only grown children. Seventeen (65 percent) of the twenty-six beginning women legislators fit this category in the 1970s. The number of first-term women legislators with one or more children under the age of eighteen increased from five (25 percent of the total) to nine (35 percent of the total). For all five of the women with young children who served before 1970, their first term would be their last. In contrast, all but two of their later counterparts served two or more terms.

Whether it was manageable, appropriate, or even moral for a woman with young children to seek and serve in public office continued to be an issue in the 1970s. One-term Senator Pamela Holand of Fargo, in making her first bid for a legislative seat in 1972, had been advised not to picture her five young children in her campaign brochure. She did and,

Pamela Holand of Fargo had five children under the age of eighteen when she sought and won a seat in the Senate in 1974. The 1970s saw an increase in the number of women legislators with young children. Credit: State Historical Society of North Dakota

whether or not that decision affected the outcome of the election, she lost her bid.[22] According to Holand, one of the special problems that women who are legislators and mothers faced was "coping with the guilt and stress associated with being in a nontraditional role."[23] Rosie Black, who had three children under the age of four when she first won election to the House in 1976, found that there were "some bad feelings from a few people about a woman who will leave a young family to serve, but for the most part, people were good about it."[24] Perhaps Bonnie Heinrich, who had a thirteen year old child when she first took a legislative seat in 1977, best summed up the experience of women like herself when she wrote, "[women] who have younger children have real problems being legislators."[25]

Many women continued to delay political careers until their children were grown or well into their teens. Shirley Lee of Turtle Lake, who had three grown children and a sixteen year old when she entered the Senate in 1972, stated in an interview shortly after her first election that the unique role of women to influence and motivate their children was "a great opportunity not to be neglected." Women's advantage she concluded was that "later on in life when their children grow up, they have more spare time than men, who must earn a living." Elynor Hendrickson of Grand Forks had three grown children who had left home by the time she first won election to the House in 1972. She recognized that "there is a time in life when a woman can become 'quite stagnant'" and that one answer for women at this stage in life is "they can run for office."[26] Ruth Meiers, first elected in 1974, also delayed her entry into politics until her children, in this case six sons, were grown. Meiers, for whom service in the legislature was a stepping stone to becoming North Dakota's first woman lieutenant governor, was quoted as saying, "I don't think I'd have been elected to the Legislature if my children hadn't have been grown." However, she saw this pattern changing for young women seeking and winning political office in the 1980s. She hoped that she had played a part in bringing about that change.[27] Most, if not all, would agree that she had.

Occupation When First Elected to the Legislature and Educational Background

The occupational profile of beginning women legislators also underwent changes in the 1970s. A significant majority of the women legislators before 1970 were employed outside the home and in occupations generally considered nontraditional. The 1970s brought a marked increase in the

The 1970s brought to legislative service more full-time homemakers, one of whom was Burness Reed of Grand Forks. Credit: State Historical Society of North Dakota

number of full-time homemakers and of women employed in traditional occupations within the ranks of first-term female legislators. The number of full-time homemakers increased from four before 1970 to nine in the Seventies. When Burness Reed of Grand Forks bid for a legislative seat in 1972, she ran as a housewife and homemaker out of the belief that "that group is currently under-represented in Bismarck."[28] Upon their first election, none of the women who served between 1923 and 1969 were teaching school or working in a health-related field. In contrast, seven women of the 1970s were engaged in one of these two fields. The number of women who worked as secretaries remained fairly constant (one before 1970 and two in the Seventies).

The occupational profile of North Dakota's women legislators broadened in the '70s with the election of a student, Terry Irving of Grand Forks. Credit: State Historical Society of North Dakota

In the Seventies the number of incoming women legislators who were employed in nontraditional occupations declined. For example, the number of women engaged in either farming or journalism decreased from nine to three. Of the other nontraditional occupations represented by one or more pioneer women legislators—banking, insurance, and sales—only sales continued to be represented in the 1970s.

In addition to the above change, the occupational profile of women beginning their legislative service in the 1970s broadened to include retired women (Marjorie Kermott of Minot and Stella Fritzell of Grand Forks) and a female student (Terry Irving). Though no lawyers were among the women who entered the legislature in the Seventies, Terry Irving was a law student when she was elected in a special election in 1973.

As in the period before 1970, the women who began their legislative service in the Seventies ranged broadly in educational background. Furthermore, they continued the primary educational pattern which was the predominance of post-high school education. Change did occur, however, in the number of women aggregated at some educational levels. While seven women who served between 1923 and 1969 attended or completed high school and two had some college work, two women who became legislators in the Seventies had a high school education and eleven had some college work. The number of college graduates among first-term women legislators increased slightly (eleven before 1970 and thirteen in the 1970s). Where the greatest change occurred was in the number of female legislators with graduate degrees. While only one woman possessed a graduate degree before 1970, during the Seventies four first-term women lawmakers had or were earning graduate degrees. The number of women with some graduate work decreased slightly (three before 1970 and two during the Seventies). The rise in the educational level of beginning women legislators during the Seventies corresponded with an increase in the educational level of the entire population.

Ethnic Background and Religious Preference

The ethnic makeup of first-term women legislators shifted in the 1970s. While nine (53 percent) of the seventeen women who entered the North Dakota legislature before 1970 and who can be identified in terms of ethnic background claimed one or more parents of Scandinavian ancestry, their counterparts among the twenty-six women first elected in the Seventies numbered eleven (42 percent), a decline of 11 percent. Gaining in representation were women of British Isles ancestry (up 17 percent to 58 percent of the total) and of

German descent (up 11 percent to 35 percent of the total). The 1970s brought the election of two women who were Germans from Russia as well as women from a variety of other ethnic backgrounds, including French, Dutch, Czech or Bohemian, and Italian. Also winning election was a woman who was part Native American. The broad ethnic diversity of the state's population as a whole was reflected to a greater extent in the Seventies than in the previous five decades.

While the ethnic makeup of beginning women legislators shifted and broadened during the Seventies, its related biographical variable, religious preference, changed little. Protestants still outnumbered members of any other faiths and Lutheranism continued to be the best represented Protestant denomination. While seventeen (65 percent) of the twenty-six women were Protestants, only four (15 percent) were Catholics. Of the remaining women, one identified herself as a Christian, one indicated her religious preference to be Reform Judaism, and two indicated no religious preference.

Family Political Connections and Prior Political Experience

While family political connections and prior political experience continued to be important to would-be women legislators in the Seventies, several significant changes had occurred in this particular pattern. During the five decades before 1970, eight (40 percent) of the twenty pioneer women legislators held prior elective office, almost exclusively as school board members or as county superintendents of schools. In contrast, only two (8 percent) of the twenty-six women who commenced their legislative careers in the Seventies held an elective office before entering the legislature. These women were Stella Fritzell, who had served on the Grand Forks park board, and Florenz Bjornson, who had served on the West Fargo school board. Previous officeholding, though a common and predictable stepping stone to the legislature for would-be

The failure of the revised state constitution in 1972 led Constitutional Convention delegates Elynor Hendrickson (left) and Stella Fritzell to run for the legislature. Credit: State Historical Society of North Dakota

women lawmakers before 1970, particularly at the school district level, was a route few women took to the legislature in the Seventies.

Two of the twenty-six novice female legislators took advantage of a rare and unusual elective opportunity which ultimately led each of them to run for the legislature. Stella Fritzell and Elynor Hendrickson, both of Grand Forks, were delegates to the State Constitutional Convention, which met for thirty days in January and February of 1972 to draft a revised state constitution. After voters turned down the proposed constitution on April 28, 1972,[29] both Fritzell and Hendrickson decided to become legislative candidates. For Fritzell the failure of the revised constitution meant the defeat of a series of environmental protection provisions for

91

Dayle Deitz, like most women legislators serving in the '70s, worked for the election of other candidates before seeking public office herself. Credit: State Historical Society of North Dakota

which she had fought. Seeking an opportunity to continue to work for these provisions, Fritzell ran for the Senate in the fall of 1972 and won.[30] Hendrickson sought election to the House that same fall, hoping to be "able to work for the implementation of 'the many sections of the proposed constitution which were designed to improve the operation of our state government and the welfare and rights of our citizens.' "[31] She also won.

Although she was not a delegate to the convention, Pamela Holand attended many of the meetings and was disappointed when the proposed constitution was rejected. Motivated to work for the passage of recommendations made in the constitution, Holand also ran for the legislature in the fall of 1972. Defeated in that election, she ran again in 1974 and won.[32]

Like the women who served in the legislature in the five decades before 1970, the twenty-six women who entered the legislature in the 1970s were active in precinct, district, and/or state party politics before they won legislative seats. Over 65 percent of these women served on campaign committees and as general party workers before becoming legislative candidates. Dayle Dietz of Wahpeton recalled "phoning, baking cookies, decorating for banquets, going door-to-door, making signs, etc." on behalf of other candidates before making her own bid for the legislature.[33] Among other things future female legislators stuffed envelopes and solicited funds, opened their homes to tours, attended state political conventions, and worked at the polls. Not nearly as many women were involved in leadership positions as were carrying on general party work. Only half as many beginning women legislators (35 percent) were elected or appointed to political party leadership positions such as state, district, and precinct chairwoman and vice chairwoman, district secretary and treasurer, and national political convention delegate.

At least a third of the women joined and worked in district and state political party women's organizations before running for the legislature. Such women's organizations had also provided a political outlet for the women who served before them. In addition, a number of the women took advantage of outlets that were either not available to or not sought by would-be women legislators in previous decades. One of these outlets was young people's political organizations. At age eleven future House member Cheryl Watkins of Fargo formed a teenage Republican group in her Minnesota community.[34] Future senator Shirley Lee was active in the Burleigh County Young Republicans and Rosie Black was involved in the young Republicans' organization in Grand

Forks.[35]

Another outlet was paid employment on the staff of an elected official in state or federal government or the staff of the legislature. Among the women to gain political know-how and experience via this route were Corliss Mushik, LuGale Backlin, Terry Irving, and Patricia "Tish" Kelly. More than a decade before she made her first bid for the legislature in 1966, Corliss Mushik worked for the legislature as a stenographer. Later she worked as a secretary to long-time political leader Arthur A. Link when he was Speaker of the House and then House minority leader.[36] LuGale Backlin of Bismarck

Carolyn Houman of Westhope was one of thirteen women who came to legislative service in the 1970s with a family tradition of officeholding. Credit: State Historical Society of North Dakota

was a committee clerk during the 1969 and 1971 sessions before her bid for a House seat in 1972.[37] Terry Irving was a legislative intern in the 1973 session.[38] She was subsequently elected to the House of Representatives in a special election in December 1973. Patricia "Tish" Kelly of Fargo worked as a staff person for two congressmen before moving to North Dakota and ultimately running for the legislature.[39]

Like a majority of the women who served in the legislature before the 1970s, half of the women who entered the legislature in the Seventies claimed family roots in electoral politics. The most common family link was a father or a husband who had served in public office at some time before the woman's legislative service. Occasionally it was a grandfather, an uncle, or father-in-law who was the former officeholder. Included in this group of male relatives were state's attorneys, school board members, city council members, a county commissioner, a register of deeds, a mayor, and a lieutenant governor.

While four women legislators before 1970 had an immediate family member or an in-law who preceded them in the legislature, seven women who entered the legislature in the Seventies could make this claim. Shirley Lee of Turtle Lake, Carolyn Houmann of Westhope, and Ruth Meiers of Ross had fathers who had been in the legislature before them. Meiers, whose first session was in 1975, took her place in the House "20 years to the day after her father finished his 22-year-career in the Legislature."[40] Janet Wentz and Pamela Holand both had in-laws who had been in the state legislature. In 1977 Jean Herman of Fargo followed in the footsteps of her husband, a five-term legislator, and Pauline Benedict succeeded her deceased husband in the same year.

The sense of inherited political interest and activism of the pre-1970 decades carried over into the 1970s. At the age of four Terry Irving stuffed envelopes with her parents for Harry Truman.[41] Violetta LaGrave shared her father's, her

95

husband's, and her son's interest in politics, a pursuit she referred to as "the love of our families."[42] In a 1985 interview Ruth Meiers recalled of her growing up years, "We literally had politics at the table with our bread and butter."[43] In an earlier interview Meiers speculated that having had a father in the Senate "probably had something to do with why I ran for the House." She recalled visiting her father in the Capitol as a child and being "impressed that Brynhild Haugland was the only woman in the House."[44] Perhaps it was part of her political inheritance that as an adult she would become one of Haugland's colleagues.

Organizational Affiliations

Like the women who preceded them, the twenty-six women who entered the legislature in the Seventies were active in a broad range of organizations, including political, professional, public service and public affairs, religious, farm, social and cultural, sororial, and patriotic. The professional organizations of which they were members, the North Dakota Nurses Association, American Agri-women, and the North Dakota Association of Realtors, to mention a few, reflected the occupational profile of this group of women. Nearly three-quarters of these women were active in four or more organizations upon their initial election to the legislature.

The most striking feature of the organizational profile of this group of women was the frequency with which they listed the League of Women Voters in their active memberships and the credit they consistently gave the League for preparing and motivating them to seek legislative office. Over a quarter of the twenty-six women were active in the League of Women Voters when they decided to make a bid for the legislature. Among these women was Corliss Mushik, whose interest in politics and government as well as specific issues was spawned by the League.[45] Mushik held several positions of responsibility in the League, including legislative lobbyist, before resigning from leadership in that organization to seek a place in the partisan world of legislative politics. Armed with a confidence in herself gained in part from her League experience, Mushik ran unsuccessfully in 1966 and 1968 as what some considered a "forlorn hope candidate" in a district where few believed a woman candidate could win. In 1970, on her third attempt, Mushik did win.[46]

Her affiliation with the League of Women Voters and her church women's group played a role in Janet Wentz's

The failed ratification of the Equal Rights Amendment in the state legislature in 1973 and the rise of the women's movement influenced Janet Wentz of Minot to bid for a seat in the House. Credit: State Historical Society of North Dakota

decision to run for the legislature. During the 1973 session Wentz, who hails from Minot, traveled to Bismarck to lobby as a member of the League of Women Voters on behalf of the Equal Rights Amendment. Despite her efforts all the Minot Republican legislators whom she had lobbied voted against the amendment and it lost by one vote. Sometime later, at a meeting of her church women's group, she relayed the story of her unsuccessful lobbying effort, spontaneously adding, "I'm as smart as those men down there." "You sure are," responded a friend. According to Wentz, this gesture of support in particular and the women's movement in general were the impetus for her seeking a legislative seat.[47]

Among the other women to take the League of Women Voters route to the legislature in the 1970s were Elynor Hendrickson and Pamela Holand. An interim step for both of them was the State Constitutional Convention. While Hendrickson, an active League member, attended as a delegate, Holand observed the proceedings as a member of the North Dakota League of Women Voters, which studied the convention as one of its official projects.

Legislative Interests

Following in the footsteps of the women they succeeded, the new crop of female legislators in the 1970s were particularly interested in education. Over half declared that education ranked among their top legislative interests. Among the educational programs that these beginning women legislators came prepared to support were public kindergarten and public television. Perhaps Kay Cann of Fargo best expressed the enthusiasm of this group of women for education when she said during her first legislative campaign in 1972, "Education is the answer to everything. . . . I would get on all the education committees I can."[48]

The welfare of people, a common interest among North Dakota's early women legislators, continued to be a central issue for female legislators after 1970. When Ruth Meiers

Environmental protection, an issue which captured the attention of an increasing number of women legislators in the 70s, had a champion in Kay Cann of Fargo. Credit: State Historical Society of NorthDakota

declared in a 1977 interview, "I'm very concerned about the needs of people,"[49] she spoke for a majority of the women who entered the legislature in the 1970s. Beginning women lawmakers expressed concern for the welfare of specific groups of people, including women, children, the elderly, Native Americans, and the underprivileged or, in the words of Representative Janet Wentz, "those in society who have the least power."[50] For some of these women, concern for the welfare of women extended to concern for their rights and support for ratification of the Equal Rights Amendment. New women legislators also demonstrated an active interest in

99

the rights of other groups of people, including workers, consumers, children, and senior citizens.

Like their predecessors, these women were interested in a variety of health care, legal, economic, and agricultural issues. More women expressed an interest in environmental issues than in the previous decades. This shift is understandable given the marked increase in energy development in the Seventies and the corresponding increase in concern over its impact. Among the beginning female legislators with an avowed interest in the environment were Stella Fritzell and Kay Cann. Fritzell, who was consistently described as the legislature's top environmentalist during her tenure, declared exploitation of natural resources to be her paramount concern from the time of her first bid for a Senate seat in 1972.[51] Cann, also an outspoken environmentalist, stated in her 1974 legislative campaign, "I grew up in northern Minnesota and watched the mining companies rape the range. I would like to have a part in seeing that this does not happen in North Dakota."[52]

Committee Assignments

The two most notable features of women's service on standing committees in the first three decades of women's participation in the North Dakota legislature were the heavy concentration of women on committees that handled education, health, and welfare and the relative absence of women on committees dealing with appropriations, taxation, agriculture, and other policy areas traditionally defined as male. A shift began to develop, however, after legislative reorganization in 1947. Though women's representation remained low on Appropriations, Agriculture, and Finance and Taxation, the overall percentage of their assignments to several other traditionally male committees increased in the Fifties and Sixties. While this shift was occurring, women continued to be assigned consistently to education and social welfare committees.

Denied her request for a seat on the Senate Education Committee as a freshman legislator in 1977, Bonnie Miller Heinrich became, in the '80s, the first woman to chair that committee. Credit: The Bismarck Tribune

A survey of the collective committee assignments of the thirty-one women who served in the legislature in the 1970s shows a shift in the pattern of women's representation on traditionally female committees, specifically, a decline in the representation of women on Education. Whereas 80 percent of those women between 1923 and 1946 and 73 percent of those between 1947 and 1969 were seated on Education, only 26 percent (or eight) of the Seventies women were assigned to this committee. Even with this decrease in female representation, Education was the fourth most frequently assigned of the twelve standing committees.

Newcomer Bonnie Miller Heinrich of Bismarck was denied placement on Education during the decade. Upon entering the legislature in 1977, Heinrich, a former teacher and a former lobbyist for the North Dakota Education Association, requested assignment to the Senate Education committee. When the Republican majority denied her request, Heinrich expressed her displeasure and fellow Democrats called the move an attempt to "spike a promising career." Republicans claimed that the denial was necessary to achieve geographic balance on the committee. Regardless of the explanation, this is a concrete example of a committee request not being honored, but more importantly, it is an example of one woman's willingness to put herself at "the center of a scrap over committee assignments."[53]

While the percentage of women legislators assigned to Education declined appreciably in the 1970s, women's representation on other traditionally female committees varied only slightly. Whereas 55 percent of the women in the legislature between 1947 and 1969 were assigned to the social welfare committee, 52 percent of those between 1970 and 1979 were assigned to this committee. Regardless of this insignificant decline, the social welfare committee was the one most frequently assigned to women during the decade. Women's representation on Political Subdivisions improved incrementally during the Seventies. Whereas three (27 percent) of the women who served in the legislature between 1947 and 1969 were seated on this committee, nine (29 percent) of their colleagues received similar assignments during the following decade.

The shift toward higher representation by women on nontraditional committees that began between 1947 and 1969 continued during the Seventies. With ten women (32 percent of the total) assigned to Judiciary during the decade, it continued to be the traditionally male committee most frequently assigned to female legislators. State and Federal Government maintained its place as the second most frequently assigned "male" committee with seven women (23 percent of the total) assigned to it between 1970 and 1979.

Committees with the lowest female representation between 1947 and 1969 continued to be those with the lowest in the 1970s. However, even these committees saw some increase in the number of women. Committees to which only one or two women were assigned in the Fifties and Sixties (Appropriations, Natural Resources, Transportation, Agriculture, Industry and Business, and Finance and Taxation) were assigned to between two and six women in the following decade. The lowest representation was on Transportation, with two women assigned, and Agriculture and Finance and Taxation, with three women each. Slightly higher gains were made in the representation of women on Appropriations, Natural Resources, and Industry, Business, and Labor, with four, five, and six women assigned to these committees respectively. The increase in women on Natural Resources is likely linked to the heightened interest of women legislators in resources development and environmental protection. Increased representation by women on Industry, Business, and Labor may be attributed to the reorganization of that committee in the early Seventies to include labor. Labor Relations was one of the committees that gained in female representation during the previous period.

The increased representation by women on Appropriations, a committee often prefaced with such words as "weighty" and "powerful," did not go unnoticed by male legislative colleagues. According to Corliss Mushik, when she and fellow newcomer, Aloha Eagles, were first appointed to House Appropriations in 1975, male committee members "patronized and spoon-fed [them] for a few weeks." In the process of challenging this attitude, the women, in Mushik's words, "revealed that females can have a firm inner core," and that, in general, they "are far less prone to depend on the back scratching system."[54] Mushik requested and received appointment to Appropriations after experiencing the frustration of seeing that committee kill bills approved in her two previous committee assignments, Education and Social Welfare.[55] Mushik, a Democrat, and Eagles, a Republican, both came to Appropriations with a demonstrated interest in

Stella Fritzell, an avid hunter and an ardent environmentalist, served on the Senate Natural Resources Committee before becoming the first woman to win a seat on Senate Appropriations. Courtesy: Sara Hanhan

"people issues." This propensity often earned them the title "bleeding hearts" and led to at least one eulogy on the House floor about their "hearts of gold."[56] Mushik and Eagles, who served on House Appropriations during the 1975, 1977, and 1979 sessions, were joined by Patricia "Tish" Kelly, a Democrat, during the 1977 session, when an equal number of Republicans and Democrats served in the House. Kelly lost her seat on Appropriations when Republicans gained control of the House in 1979. She was placed, however, on the "important House Finance and Taxation Committee."[57]

Until 1979 the few women who had been appointed to Appropriations all served in the House of Representatives. The 1979 session saw the first woman assigned to Senate Appropriations, referred to in the *Grand Forks Herald* as "the most exclusive committee of the most exclusive men's club in the state." The woman was Stella Fritzell. In an interview conducted at the time of her appointment Fritzell indicated that the reason she was given Senate Appropriations was, "I asked for it." In addition to wanting to be involved in economic issues, Fritzell sought the move to Appropriations because she felt that her reputation as an ardent environmentalist had weakened her position on Natural Resources, her committee of choice for the preceding three sessions. In surrendering her position on Natural Resources, Fritzell remarked, "Whenever you get labeled, you lose your effectiveness."[58]

The only standing committee on which no women served during the Seventies was Joint Constitutional Revision. This committee, which is comprised of members from both houses, was not established until 1977.

The development of female committee assignments is illustrated in table 3. The increase in the number of women in the legislature in the Seventies over the number in the two earlier time periods accounts for the greater number of total committee assignments. As the table indicates, however, this increase had little effect on the proportion of assignments to traditionally female and traditionally male committees. The shift toward greater representation by women on "male" committees that occurred between 1947 and 1969 clearly continued in the Seventies. The result of this shift was that by the end of the sixth decade of their service in the North Dakota legislature, women were as likely to be addressing nontraditional policy domains by virtue of their committee assignments as they were traditional.

Table 3.—Committee assignments, 1923-1979

Periods & (total No. of assignments)	No. & (%) to trad. female	No. & (%) to trad. male
1923-1946 (52)	37 (71)	15 (29)
1947-1969 (35)	16 (46)	19 (54)
1970-1979 (73)	33 (45)	40 (55)
1980-1989 ___		

Committee Chairs and Other Leadership Positions

In the five decades before 1970, four of North Dakota's women legislators chaired standing committees and two served as vice chairs. Only one woman, Minnie Craig, was selected for a leadership position other than committee chair or vice chair. In this case, the exception to the rule was a notable one in that Craig was elected to the highest position in the House. While gains were made in the 1970s, the pattern of underrepresentation of women in legislative leadership positions continued.

Between 1970 and 1979 only one woman, Brynhild Haugland, a House Republican, chaired a standing committee. She chaired the social welfare committee throughout the decade, including the 1977 session when Republicans and Democrats shared control of the House.

Women legislators have fared better in attaining secondary leadership positions on standing committees. Eight women served as vice chairs during the Seventies, six in the House and two in the Senate. One woman, Fern Lee of Towner, was vice chair of two committees during the decade, bringing the number of positions held to nine. Seven out of eight of the female vice chairs were Republicans. The lone Democrat, Anna Powers, was vice chair of State and Federal Government during the 1977 session when Democrats had

Corliss Mushik, who became assistant minority leader in the House in 1977, was the first woman to hold this position in either chamber. She was also the first female assistant majority leader. Credit: State Historical Society of North Dakota

an equal say with Republicans. The other women who attained vice chair positions were Grace Stone (House Judiciary in 1971 and 1973), Aloha Eagles (House Social Welfare in 1971 and 1973), Fern Lee (House Political Subdivisions in 1975 and House State and Federal Government in 1979), Shirley Lee (Senate Natural Resources in 1975, 1977, and 1979), Stella Fritzell (Senate Industry, Business, and Labor in 1977), Alice Olson (House Social Welfare in 1977 and 1979), and Rosie Black (House Political Subdivisions in 1979).

Three women served in leadership positions other than committee chair or vice chair: one as assistant minority leader in the House, one as Democratic caucus chair in the House, and one was Democratic caucus chair in the Senate. Each was the first woman to serve in that capacity in the North Dakota legislature. All were Democrats.

When Corliss Mushik was serving her first term as assistant minority leader in the House in 1977, the press referred to her as "a bulwark of the Democratic party in the North Dakota House."[59] She went on to serve as the second in command of the Democratic minority in the House for an-

Joann McCaffrey of Grand Forks identified women's "minority attitude" as one of the special problems facing female legislators in the '70s. Credit: State Historical Society of North Dakota

other two sessions. Gaining the confidence of fellow House Democrats and selection as one of their floor leaders were particularly rewarding experiences for this Mandan legislator.[60]

Terry Irving of Grand Forks was a freshman legislator when she was selected by House Democrats as their caucus chair during the legislative presession in December 1974. At the time Irving credited her successful bid for the position to the fact that she was a woman and that she was from a larger city.[61] In retrospect, Irving thought that her election as House Democratic caucus chair was her major accomplishment as a legislator.[62] When Senate Democrats selected Bonnie Miller Heinrich as their caucus leader in December 1978, she had just been elected to her second term in the legislature.

While seniority and party affiliation are important factors when legislative leadership positions are being contested, some have named gender as another contributing factor. Jeane Kirkpatrick and Irene Diamond have observed a preponderance of men in the top leadership positions in legislative bodies. The "old boys' club," experienced if not named by early female legislative leader Minnie Craig, was still alive and well in the 1970s according to some of the women who served during the decade. At the time of the 1984 election when her name was on the ballot for lieutenant governor, Ruth Meiers recalled that when she was a rookie legislator in the 1970s the "old boys' club was very strong, very definite."[63] According to Corliss Mushik in a 1979 interview, it was a club to which women did not belong.[64] Rosie Black found not fitting in with the "old boys" and "young turks"[65] an isolating experience. Among the other problems that women legislators reported were a lack of respect from some male colleagues,[66] a sense of either not being heard[67] or not being taken seriously,[68] a lack of understanding of the "undercurrents" and "power plays" familiar to male legislators,[69] and the bewilderment of being so outnumbered by men.[70] One female legislator recalled that the most difficult thing about her one term in the House was "working around arrogant, obnoxious, sexist creeps with no sense of humor."[71] Coupled with these problems was what Joann McCaffrey of Grand Forks, who served a single term in 1977, described as women's tendency to "hold a 'minority attitude' toward themselves and other women" demonstrated when they "lack self confidence and independent faith in their own abilities."[72] McCaffrey's opinion was echoed by fellow House member Janet Wentz, when she wrote:

"Our strengths are also our weaknesses. We lack self confidence. We are too polite. We are not assertive enough. We are hung up on being fair. All of these things put us at a disadvantage in a male system and politics is so male—so much the 'old boy' network."[73]

Sponsored Legislation

While the twenty women who were in the North Dakota legislature during the five decades before 1970 were involved 576 times in sponsoring bills and resolutions, the thirty-one women of the 1970s were involved in 738 such sponsorships. Two reasons for the higher rate of legislative sponsorships in the latter period were the significant increase in the number of women and the greater proportion of these women who held multiple terms. Legislative sponsorships outnumbered actual pieces of sponsored legislation because more than one woman sponsored many of the latter.

The vast majority (71 percent) of legislative sponsorships that women made between 1923 and 1969 addressed issues and concerns conventionally viewed as male, while only slightly over one-fourth (26 percent) addressed traditionally women's issues and just 3 percent spoke to issues that affected women as a class. While the number of sponsorships in the first category remained high in the 1970s (460 or 62 percent of the total), the overall proportion decreased nine percentage points. In turn, the number of sponsorships in the categories of traditionally women's issues and women's class issues rose to 225 (31 percent of the total) and fifty-three (7 percent of the total), respectively.

As in the previous period, the female legislation sponsored in nontraditional or "male" policy areas covered a wide range of subject matters, with agriculture, election and campaign reform, licensing, taxes, legislative reform, banking, and insurance continuing to be among the most common. Women legislators demonstrated their interest in the rights of senior citizens, consumers, mobile home owners, and other groups through their sponsorship of bills designed to prohibit discrimination and extend protection. Concern for animal rights was expressed through a variety of bills, including one that defined rare and endangered animals and another that required that vehicles hauling live animals in the winter be covered. Women legislators' heightened interest in the environment was reflected in a number of bills, including one requiring all beverage containers to be recyclable and another requiring permits for and environmental impact statements from persons engaged in activities that would significantly affect environmental quality. The female lawmakers also turned their attention to energy development and its corresponding impact. Female sponsored legislation that dealt with these issues sought, among other things, to provide for a coal development impact aid program, enforce surface mine reclamation, limit the construction and operation of nuclear energy conversion facilities in the state, and create a natural resources council.

Equally diverse was the legislation that focused on those issues traditionally viewed as women's concerns—health, welfare, education, and children. While a broad range of health concerns were addressed, one of the areas that received considerable attention was drug and alcohol abuse, prevention, treatment, and education. The growing atten-

111

tion and sensitivity to rights issues surfaced in several pieces of female-sponsored legislation, including one bill that required designated nonsmoking areas in public buildings and another that called for the study of the rights of nursing home residents.

Welfare legislation considered a wide range of needs of the elderly, the handicapped, the disabled, and the poor. Women legislators sponsored proposals for a number of studies in this area that had far-reaching goals and implications. Among these was a study to determine the feasibility and potential benefits of establishing a department of human services, a study of the implementation of laws requiring public buildings and facilities to be accessible and usable for the physically handicapped, and a study that related to welfare of the state's senior citizens in terms of housing, nutrition, education, and employment.

Education legislation covered a multitude of concerns relating to students, teachers, administrators, curriculum, and facilities. Authorizing the North Dakota Educational Broadcasting Council to contract with noncommercial public television and radio stations and giving the state's school districts the authority to establish free public kindergarten were among the educational issues that women legislators championed. Female-sponsored legislation relating to school curriculum sought to integrate consumer, environmental, and Indian education into the established course of study in public schools.

Women lawmakers sponsored numerous pieces of legislation that dealt with the rights and the protection of minors. Prevention of drug and alcohol abuse among youths was the focus of many of these bills.

While only 7 percent of female legislative sponsorships involved women as a class in their roles as mothers, wives, and homemakers and in their positions in the workplace, in government, and in education, this figure represents a notable increase from the previous period. In the five decades before 1970, women legislators were involved eighteen times in sponsoring legislation in this category. Individual pieces of legislation numbered eleven. In the succeeding decade, women legislators were involved fifty-three times in such sponsorships. The number of bills and resolutions was thirty. Regardless of which measure is used, the figures indicate that issues and concerns that affected women as a class were addressed nearly three times as often by women legislators in the Seventies than in the previous five decades.

With the increase in the number of sponsorships and pieces of legislation in this area came an expansion in the issues they addressed. This phenomenon occurred not only in North Dakota, but in legislative bodies nationwide in the 1970s as "the women's movement focused public attention on a host of new issues, including rape, wife beating, sexual harassment, child care, and displaced homemakers." According to historian Susan M. Hartmann, by the end of the decade, the women's movement and its allies had worked "a modest revolution in public policy."[74]

Nineteen of the thirty pieces of legislation affecting women as a class that North Dakota's women lawmakers sponsored in the Seventies addressed issues and concerns of women in their roles as wives, mothers, and homemakers. Thirteen or two-thirds of these focused on improving the legal status of women in marriage, at widowhood, and at divorce. These bills and resolutions sought a variety of reforms relating to domicile, property, alimony, child support, inheritance, insurance, and domestic violence. A half dozen pieces of legislation addressed the question of abortion.

Legislation sought to discard remnants of English common law that viewed wives as nonpersons and to reinforce the concept of marriage as an equal partnership.[75] In 1979 Jean Herman, Rosie Black, and Aloha Eagles addressed

113

a prime example of a lingering inequity in marriage law when they introduced a bill to repeal that section of the North Dakota Century Code that designated the husband as the head of the family. Under this law the husband had the right to "choose any reasonable place and mode of living" and the wife was obliged to conform to it. Failure of the wife to do so was considered desertion.[76] In 1975 Terry Irving and Aloha Eagles sponsored a bill recognizing the wife's contributions to the support of the household through her labors as homemaker. Eagles sponsored a related bill, this one in the area of probate law, during the 1979 session. This bill recognized the equal effort of a husband and a wife in obtaining property owned in joint tenancy and affirmed the inheritance rights of the surviving spouse upon the death of the other. A bill Corliss Mushik sponsored during the same session raised the problem of domestic violence and affirmed the right of the abused spouse to protection and relief. In 1975 Cheryl Watkins and Janet Wentz introduced a bill designed to protect the rights of rape victims in criminal prosecutions. The bill did not address spousal rape, an issue that would surface during the following decade.

Legislation that dealt with the legal status of women at widowhood and at divorce sought to provide economic protections for homemakers upon the loss of a spouse through death or divorce. In 1977 and 1979 female lawmakers introduced four separate pieces of legislation to reform divorce laws in relation to alimony, child support, and the division of property. In 1973 Cheryl Watkins sponsored a bill that reduced the incidence of nonpayment of court-ordered child support. In 1977 Corliss Mushik, Janet Wentz, Aloha Eagles, and Pauline Benedict sponsored a resolution directing an interim study to determine the extent of the displaced homemaker crisis in North Dakota and to identify available programs and services. During the following session Mushik and Alice Olson sponsored a bill to provide counseling, training, jobs, services, and health care for women who had

Cheryl Watkins was among the women legislators serving in the 1970s to introduce legislation designed to reform the state's child custody and support laws. Credit: State Historical Society of North Dakota

been displaced from their traditional roles as mothers and wives by death, divorce, or other loss of family income. In 1973 LuGale Backlin sponsored legislation that addressed the health care and insurance needs of a specific group of homemakers, single mothers.

The issue of abortion continued into the 1970s. In the 1971 session Aloha Eagles again sponsored a bill to liberalize North Dakota's abortion laws (co-sponsored by Grace Stone). Just before the defeat of the bill on the House floor in February 1971, Eagles predicted that if the bill did not pass, the "courts will do what the Legislature didn't have the vision to do."[77] In January 1973 the United States Supreme Court restricted the authority of state legislatures to prohibit abortion through its controversial decision in the case of Roe v. Wade. Beginning in the 1973 session and continuing throughout the decade, legislation seeking to limit the effects of Roe v. Wade was introduced in the North Dakota legislature. One or more women sponsored five of these bills and resolutions.

Eleven of the thirty pieces of women-as-a-class legislation focused on women in their positions in the workplace, in government, and in education. While the majority of these bills and resolutions sought to expand the rights of women and to prohibit discrimination against women, several measures were drafted in opposition to the broadest of the antidiscrimination measures, the Equal Rights Amendment.

In 1975 Terry Irving was the sole sponsor of a bill that directed an interim study of state laws which discriminated on the basis of sex. Women legislators in the Seventies sponsored measures designed to identify and address specific areas of sex and other discrimination. A bill which Marjorie Kermott, Grace Stone, Fern Lee, and Brynhild Haugland sponsored in 1973 sought to further erode sex discrimination in the state's political party system by adding a vice chairwoman as an office to district and state committees. In 1975 Corliss Mushik, Terry Irving, and Cheryl Watkins introduced a bill that would ban pay toilets in public establishments. Such facilities were viewed as discriminating against women as well as the elderly, the poor, and the young.[78] Stella Fritzell in 1977 and Ruth Meiers in 1979 sponsored bills against discriminatory interment and insurance practices. In 1979 Jean Herman and Aloha Eagles' bill prohibited discrimination in employment because of sex, race, religion, national origin, age, or marital status, and Eagles and Corliss Mushik sponsored a measure that would provide for a women's detention facility in conjunction with the state penitentiary.

Beginning in 1973 and continuing throughout the decade, the North Dakota legislature debated the broadest measure aimed at prohibiting sex discrimination, the Equal Rights Amendment (ERA), which stated, "Equality of rights under the law shall not be denied or abridged by the United States or by any State on account of sex."[79] First introduced to the United States Congress in 1923, Congress finally approved the ERA on March 22, 1972 and it was sent to state legislatures for ratification.[80] In 1973 Aloha Eagles and Elynor Hendrickson called for North Dakota's ratification of the amendment through a House resolution. This and a comparable Senate resolution failed to pass. When the legislature approved ratification of the ERA in 1975, the resolution originated in the Senate with no female sponsors. During that session the Senate requested a study of the effects of the proposed amendment. Fern Lee sponsored the resolution, which failed. Resolutions rescinding the state's ratification of the ERA were introduced in the Senate in 1977 with Shirley Lee as a sponsor and in the House in 1979 with Fern Lee as a sponsor. These failed as well, and the Seventies ended with North Dakota among those states which supported the adoption of a federal equal rights amendment.

Summary and Conclusion

When the Seventies began, five women were serving in the North Dakota legislature, all in the House. By the end of the decade twenty women were in the legislature, seventeen in the House and three in the Senate. This substantial increase in the number of female legislators signaled other broad changes in the collective profile of "political woman" as she emerged as a force in the state's legislature in the 1970s.

While female legislators continued to be concentrated in the House, some inroads were made in the Senate. Whereas

117

two women served in the Senate between 1923 and 1969, four took their places in the upper chamber during the Seventies. As Democrats continued their challenge of Republican control of the legislature, Democratic women occupied legislative seats with greater frequency. Though women from the eastern half of the state continued to outnumber those from the west, urban women came to outnumber rural and small town women, reversing the geographic pattern of the five decades before 1970. While a majority of the women between 1923 and 1969 were single-term legislators, the Seventies brought a reversal in this pattern.

The background characteristics of women who entered the legislature in the Seventies were similar in some ways to those of the women who preceded them and different in others. While the median age of first-term women legislators decreased only slightly, the range of their ages broadened to include more women in their sixties and the first women in their twenties. Though married women continued to predominate, the marital profile of first-term women legislators broadened to include divorced women. While the percentage of beginning women legislators with no active child-rearing responsibilities remained high, more women with young children sought and won election to the legislature. Though some women continued to delay their political ambitions until after their children were grown and those with young children commonly experienced guilt and other difficulties, being a mother of young children was less of a deterrent to would-be female legislators in the Seventies than it had been in the previous five decades.

One of the most significant shifts was in the occupational profile of novice women legislators. Whereas a majority of the women who served between 1923 and 1969 were employed in occupations generally considered nontraditional, women who entered the legislature in the Seventies were more likely to be full-time homemakers or employed in traditional occupations such as teaching and nursing. Nontraditional for their time in several respects, including profession, North Dakota's pioneer female legislators paved the way for women with more conventional occupational pursuits. The Seventies also brought a broadening of the occupational profile of incoming women legislators to include students and retired persons.

Like their predecessors, women first elected in the Seventies commonly sought post-high school education. With greater frequency, they earned undergraduate and graduate degrees.

The 1970s brought a shift in ethnic background. More ethnically diverse than the women who served before 1970, the new crop of female legislators included women of French, Dutch, Czech, Italian, Russian-German, German, British Isles, Scandinavian, and Native American ancestry. Women of British Isles ancestry outnumbered Scandinavians, previously the dominant ethnic group among incoming female legislators.

While the ethnic makeup of beginning women legislators broadened, their religious background remained consistent. Protestants, most of them Lutherans, continued to outnumber members of other faiths.

Several changes occurred in relation to family political connections and previous political experience. Prior officeholding, a common stepping stone to the legislature for women before 1970, was rare among those women who first won seats in the Seventies. They were more likely to pursue other opportunities in politics that prepared them to bid for legislative duty, including paid employment in government. While nearly two-thirds were active as campaign and general party workers, just over one-third held leadership positions in their respective political parties. It continued to be common for women legislators to have a relative, most typically a father or husband, who preceded them in elective office.

Like the women who came before them, women entering the legislature in the 1970s were active in a wide range of political and other organizations. Membership in the League of Women Voters, which led at least one pioneer female lawmaker to the legislature, figured in the prelegislative experience of over a quarter of the women newly elected in the Seventies.

Though education and public welfare continued to be the interests most commonly shared by North Dakota's female legislators, women first elected in the Seventies, like their predecessors, were concerned about a wide range of issues. Among these were environmental protection and resources development, two of the issues which dominated the decade. The shift toward greater female representation on traditionally male committees that began after legislative reorganization in 1947 continued into the Seventies. While women legislators, newcomers and veterans alike, continued to be assigned with considerable frequency to standing education and welfare committees, the percentage of women assigned to Education notably declined. The committee women were most often assigned to was the social welfare committee.

Though women legislators in the Seventies were underrepresented in leadership positions, they did make gains over their predecessors. While only one woman chaired a standing committee during the decade, eight women were vice chairs. Four women had served as committee chairs and two as vice chairs during the previous five decades. Whereas Minnie Craig was the only woman to be elected to a leadership position other than committee chair or vice chair before 1970, three women rose to other leadership positions in the legislative hierarchy in the Seventies.

Although women in the Seventies had a higher rate of legislative sponsorships than the women who served before 1970, they, like their predecessors, concentrated their bill-

and-resolution-making activity in those policy areas traditionally viewed as male. Just over 30 percent of their legislative sponsorships addressed issues traditionally viewed as female, while 7 percent spoke to issues that affected women as a class. The actual number of bills and resolutions sponsored in this category was thirty. During the previous five decades, women sponsored eleven such pieces of legislation. In other words, women legislators were addressing the particular concerns of women three times as often as they had previously. A number of these bills and resolutions focused on "new" issues such as domestic violence and displaced homemakers. Some dealt with two of the most controversial issues before the legislature in the 1970s—abortion and the Equal Rights Amendment.

While owing a debt to those pioneer female legislators who proved that women have a legitimate place in the legislature, women legislators in the Seventies advanced the work of their predecessors by making their increased presence felt on committees, in leadership positions, and through their sponsored legislation. Through their service, these thirty-one women proved that "political woman" as described by Kirkpatrick and others not only existed but was a force for change in the North Dakota legislature.

Chapter 2 End Notes

[1]Kirkpatrick, 217.

[2]Aloha Eagles, "Women in North Dakota Politics," unpublished paper prepared upon the request of the North Dakota Commission on the Status of Women, 1973.

[3]Hartmann, 86-7.

[4]Mandel, 13.

[5]Ibid., 16-17.

[6]Kirkpatrick, 3.

[7]Johnson and Stanwick, xix.

[8]Mandel, 115-116.

[9]Remele, "North Dakota History," 40-41.

[10]Ibid., 39.

[11]"Women's Caucus," *Fargo Forum*, 24 January 1975.

[12]Corliss Mushik, taped interview with Corliss Mushik and Patricia "Tish" Kelly by author, 10 September 1990.

[13]Ibid.

[14]Patricia "Tish" Kelly, taped interview with Corliss Mushik and Patricia "Tish" Kelly by author, 10 September 1990.

[15]Ibid.

[16]Severson, 205.

[17]*Grand Forks Herald*, 26 November 1972, 4.

[18]"Women in Politics," *Fargo Forum*, 29 October 1972.

[19]John Dvorak, "Women Contingent," *Fargo Forum*, 26 November 1972.

[20]Sylvia Paine, "Women Out to Win," *Fargo Forum*, 27 October 1974.

[21]Pauline Benedict, telephone interview by author, 19 May 1990.

[22]"Women in Politics."

[23]Pamela Holand, "Women Legislators History Project Survey," completed 8 May 1989. Held by author.

[24]Rosie Black, "Women Legislators History Project Survey," completed 12 September 1989. Held by author.

[25]Bonnie Miller Heinrich, "Women Legislators History Project Survey," completed 4 October 1989. Held by author.

[26]Dvorak.

[27]Mike Dorsher, "Ruth Meiers' Last Interview: Historic North Dakotan talks about politics and fatal fight with cancer," *Bismarck Tribune*, 22 March 1987.

[28]"Republican ticket includes incumbents, newcomers," *Grand Forks Herald*, 20 November 1972.

[29]Marilyn Guttromson, "Historical Sketches of Major Constitutional Revision Efforts in North Dakota: 1889-1973," in *North Dakota Constitutional Convention, 1971-72: A Newspaper Account* (Bismarck: North Dakota State Library, 1974), 18-19.

[30]Jeff Blume, "Stella Fritzell: hunting solutions in North Dakota," *High Country News*, 23 March 1979, 16.

[31]"Republican ticket includes incumbents, newcomers."

[32]Holand survey.

[33]Dayle Dietz, "Women Legislators History Project Survey," completed 10 September 1989. Held by author.

[34]Cheryl Watkins, "Women Legislators History Project Survey," completed 12 October 1989. Held by author.

[35]Shirley Lee, "Women Legislators History Project Survey," completed 20 March 1989. Held by author.

[36]Lucille Hendrickson, "Newest Woman Legislator Looks at Both Sides," *Bismarck Tribune*, 1 February 1971.

[37]Judy Johnson, "Former GOP Solon Committee Clerk," *Grand Forks Herald*, 27 March 1975.

[38]"Link supports Irving candidacy," *Grand Forks Herald*, 30 November 1973.

[39]Patricia "Tish" Kelly, "Women Legislators History Project Survey," completed 18 April 1989. Held by author.

[40]Dorsher, "Ruth Meiers' Last Interview."

[41]Terry Irving, "Women Legislators History Project Survey," completed 17 May 1989. Held by author.

[42]Violetta LaGrave, "Women Legislators History Project Survey," completed 5 May 1989. Held by author.

[43]"Who's Lt. Gov? I'm she," *Bismarck Tribune*, 20 October 1985.

[44]Steve Andrist, "Little Done for People, Says Democrat," *Bismarck Tribune*, 28 March 1977.

[45]Stan Stelter, "Corliss Mushik," *Bismarck Tribune*, 23 October 1980.

[46]Corliss Mushik, "Women Legislators History Project Survey," completed [October 1989]. Held by author.

[47]Janet Wentz, "Women Legislators History Project Survey," completed 12 May 1989. Held by author.

[48]"Women in Politics."

[49]Andrist, "Little Done for People".

[50]Wentz survey.

[51]Chuck Haga, "18th District Senate Candidates Include Longtime Vets," *Grand Forks Herald*, 23 October 1972.

[52]"Mrs. Cann Seeks N.D. House Seat," *Fargo Forum*, 5 June 1974.

[53]Tim Fought, "Anger Got Her to Legislature," *Bismarck Tribune*, 3 March 1978.

[54]Mushik survey

[55]Mavis Vogel, "Local legislator is a fighter," *Mandan News*, 11 March 1979.

[56]Larry Johnson, "Appropriations 'Sidekicks' Part Once Again," *Bismarck Tribune*, 30 March 1979.

[57]"Kelly Loses Appropriations Panel Seat," *Fargo Forum*, 8 December 1978.

[58]Mike Jacobs, "Stella Fritzell: first woman on Appropriations Committee," *Grand Forks Herald*, 17 December 1978.

[59]Steve Andrist, "Mushik at Hub of Democrats' Decision-Making," *Bismarck Tribune*, 17 February 1977.

[60]Mushik survey.

[61]"Terry Irving chairs Dems House caucus," , 4 December 1974.

[62]Terry Irving, "Women Legislators History Project Survey," completed 17 May 1989. Held by author.

[63]Rebecca Hunt, "Ruth Meiers," *Bismarck Tribune*, 2 November 1984.

[64]Vogel, "Local legislator is a fighter."

[65]Black survey.

[66]Elynor Hendrickson, "Women Legislators History Project Survey," completed 20 May 1989. Held by author.

[67]Florenz Bjornson, "Women Legislators History Project Survey," completed 14 July 1989. Held by author.

[68]Burness Reed, "Women Legislators History Project Survey," completed 26 May 1989. Held by author.

[69]Sister Mary Beauclair, "Women Legislators History Project Survey," completed 22 May 1989. Held by author.

[70]Elaine Vig, "Women Legislators History Project Survey," completed 20 March 1989. Held by author.

[71]Irving survey.

[72]Joann McCaffrey, "Women Legislators History Project Survey," completed 3 April 1989. Held by author.

[73]Wentz survey.

[74]Hartmann, 99, 127.

[75]Nancy Maxwell, "And They Lived Happily Ever After?" in *The Legal Status of Homemakers in North Dakota* by the Homemakers Committee of the National Commission on the Observance of International Women's Year (Washington, D.C.: U.S. Government Printing Office, 1976), 1-2.

[76]Ibid., 2.

[77]"Death Knell was Sounded Early," *Fargo Forum*, 5 February 1971.

[78]North Dakota Legislative Council, Corliss Mushik's Testimony on HB 1363, State and Federal Government Committee Minutes, 12 February 1975, 2.

[79]Hartmann, 106.

[80]Sara M. Evans, *Born for Liberty: A History of Women in America* (New York: The Free Press, 1989), 291.

3

"Political Woman," An Established Force: The 1980s

Twenty years ago we could say with Simone de Beauvoir, "The free woman is just being born." Today she has become a force.[1]

— Eleanor Holmes Norton, 1982

How, then do we as women make a difference? As a political woman I firmly believe we have to be in positions where we can affect change—we have to seek out and accept roles of leadership where decisions are made .... Women in public life are already making a difference. Why do you think that such issues as day care facilities, nursing home care, battered wives' programs, displaced homemakers' programs, and others are finally surging forward in the nation's consciousness—because women's groups are addressing these problems—because women are lobbying for change—because women care.[2]

— Lieutenant Governor Ruth Meiers, 1986

Historical Background and Overview

The 1980 elections were distinguished by more than Ronald Reagan's rise to the presidency and the victory of a movement which had come to be referred to as the "New Right." They signaled continued change in the pattern of women's participation in politics.

Political analysts, accustomed after the Seventies to reviewing election returns for evidence of shifts in the electoral behavior of female voters, observed and reported two related developments in the aftermath of the 1980 elections. The first of these was significant differences in how women and men voted for candidates and on issues. The term "gender gap" was coined to describe this development. A second development was that women voted at the same rate

Fourteen of the eighteen women serving in the legislature during the 1983 session were House members. They were (seated left to right) Corliss Mushik, Tish Kelly, Brynhild Haugland (standing left to right) Donna Nalewaja, Dagne Olsen, Jean Rayl, Judy DeMers, Ruth Meiers, Janet Wentz, Rosie Black, Julie Hill, Alice Olson, Aloha Eagles, and Adella Williams. Courtesy: Brynhild Haugland

as men for the first time in peacetime. The 1980 elections also marked the first time that the platforms of the two major political parties differed significantly on women's issues.[3]

Though their gains were less dramatic than in the previous decade, women continued to be elected to public office at a steady rate in the 1980s. Women's representation in state legislatures increased in every election during the decade. In 1981, 908 women were serving in state legislatures, making up 12 percent of the total. By 1989 the 1,262 women who served nationwide in state legislatures represented 17 percent of the total. The vast majority of these women (1,002) held seats in the lower house of the state legislative seats.[4]

Progress in terms of numbers was less steady for North Dakota's women legislators in the 1980s. Whereas twenty women had served during the 1979 session, the number of women in the 1981 session dropped to eighteen, where it stayed for the next two sessions. The 1987 session saw a return to the twenty mark and the 1989 Centennial session brought twenty-four women to the legislature. In 1989 women accounted for 15 percent of all North Dakota legislators, an all-time high.

The total number of women who served in the North Dakota legislature in the 1980s was forty-one. Fifteen entered before 1980; twenty-six began their terms during the Eighties. Twenty-six women commenced their legislative careers in the Seventies as well. However, only five entered that decade as experienced legislators. The significant increase in veteran women legislators in the Eighties evidenced the growing seniority of female lawmakers.

With a few exceptions, major economic and political trends observed in the Seventies continued to play themselves out in the Eighties in North Dakota. The farm economy remained weak and the number of farms decreased steadily.

Energy industries, which had boomed in the previous decade, followed agriculture into a bust cycle after worldwide oil prices declined in 1981. In politics Democrats continued to challenge Republican control of state offices and the legislature. In 1980 they lost the governorship only to regain it in 1984. House Democrats outnumbered House Republicans for the second time in the state's history in 1983. In 1987

The Eighties brought an unprecedented number of Democratic women to the legislature, including Adella Williams (left) of Lidgerwood and June Enget of Powers Lake. Credit: The Bismarck Tribune

Democrats took control of the state Senate for the first time. The Eighties, the decade in which two-party politics finally took hold in North Dakota, ended with Republicans controlling the House and Democrats controlling the Senate.[5]

The more equal balance of legislative power between Republicans and Democrats in the Eighties was reflected in the numbers of first-term women legislators who were elected from the two parties. Though Democratic women had served with greater frequency in the Seventies than in the previous period, their gains among beginning female legislators in the following decade were unprecedented. Of the twenty-six women who entered the legislature between 1980 and 1989, fourteen (54 percent) were Democrats and twelve (46 percent) were Republicans. Because eleven (73 percent) of the fifteen carry-over women were Republicans, Republican women continued to outnumber Democratic women.

While women legislators continued to be concentrated in the House during the Eighties, their inroads into the

Donna Nalewaja of Fargo was one of two female House members to seek and win a seat in the Senate in the 1980s. The other was Corliss Mushik. Credit: State Historical Society of North Dakota

Senate continued as well. Twenty-three (88 percent) of the twenty-six beginning women legislators were initially elected to the House and three (12 percent) to the Senate. In 1986 one of these newcomers, Donna Nalewaja of Fargo, gave up the House seat that she had held for two sessions to run for the Senate. Her bid was successful. After serving six terms in the House, veteran legislator Corliss Mushik sought and won a seat in the upper house in 1984. With these migrations, a total of eight women came to occupy Senate seats during the Eighties, four times the number that had served between 1923 and 1969 and twice the number that had served in the Seventies. During the 1989 session five women served in the Senate, a record number.

In keeping with the geographical pattern established during the first five decades of women's service in the legislature, female lawmakers continued to come with greater frequency from eastern North Dakota. Seventeen (65 percent) of the women who entered the legislature in the Eighties came from counties east of a line dividing the state in half east to west (see figure 3). With no beginning female legislators elected from west of the Missouri River, this region remained largely unrepresented by women during the Eighties. Just over half of the women who commenced their service before 1980 were from the eastern half of the state.

The shift toward greater representation in the legislature by urban women than rural and small town women begun in the 1970s continued in the 1980s. Fifteen (58 percent) of the twenty-six novice women legislators were from the cities of Bismarck, Fargo, Grand Forks, and Minot. As in the previous decade, well over half of these urban women were from Grand Forks and Fargo. Three-fifths of the carry-over women hailed from the four cities listed above. This shift in female representation in the legislature which began in the Seventies predated and perhaps signaled a shift in the general population which the 1987 census confirmed.

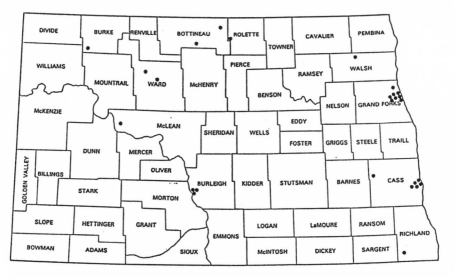

Fig. 3. Post offices of women entering the legislature in the 1980s.
(Base map: North Dakota Highway Department.)

More North Dakotans lived in cities and towns than in rural areas.[6]

Yet another pattern that underwent change in the 1970s continued in its new course in the 1980s. Though most of the women who served before 1970 were single-term legislators, less than one-third of the women who won legislative seats in the Seventies were in this group. In the Eighties single-term and multiple-term female legislators were split evenly, thirteen of each. However, over half of the women who were classified as single-term legislators began their first term in 1989.

Background Characteristics

As in the previous chapter, the discussion of background characteristics as well as legislative interests will focus on only those twenty-six women who entered the legislature in the decade under consideration. When the discussion turns to committee assignments, leadership positions, and sponsored legislation, the focus will broaden to include the fifteen women whose service began before and continued into the Eighties.

As they had heralded the first seating of women lawmakers in the North Dakota legislature in the early 1920s and the dramatic increase in their numbers in the early 1970s, the press took note of the decline in their ranks in the 1980 elections. No vestiges of the press' once intense interest in the personal backgrounds of the state's female legislators were to be found in a *Fargo Forum* article which appeared shortly after the November election. The focus of the article was numbers, as evidenced by the headline "Growth in number of N.D. women legislators comes to an end." Speculating on the reason for this reversal in trend, one male political observer explained, "Maybe this is the number of women the voters are comfortable with." A reason cited by "prominent women in both parties" was that "Women have yet to shake their image as homemakers," an image that for decades had been the focus of the press' interest in and coverage of female legislators.[7]

Age, Marital Status, and Number and Age of Children at Time of First Election to the Legislature

A decrease in the number of first-term women legislators in their forties and sixties and an increase in the number of women in their twenties and thirties resulted in an appreciable decline in the median age of beginning women legislators in the Eighties. Starting out at forty-eight during the period 1923 to 1969 and declining only slightly to forty-seven during the Seventies, the median age of incoming female legislators dropped to forty-three during the following decade. Corresponding to this drop was a steady increase in the number of new women legislators in their twenties and thirties. During the five decades before 1970 they numbered four (20 percent of the total); in the Seventies they numbered seven (27 percent of the total), and in the Eighties they numbered eleven (42 percent of the total).

134

The 1980s brought an appreciable decline in the median age of beginning women legislators. Contributing to that decline were Sarah Carlson (left) and Jennifer Ring, both of Grand Forks, who were twenty-two and twenty-eight, respectively, when first elected. Credit: Doug Van Tassel. Courtesy: The Grand Forks Herald

As Diane Larson of Bismarck could attest to,
balancing legislative service with family needs
and obligations continued to be a challenge for
women legislators in the '80s. Credit: State His-
torical Society of North Dakota

The marital profile of beginning female legislators, which expanded in the Seventies to include divorced women, continued to be dominated by married women in the 1980s. While twenty-one (81 percent) of the twenty-six women who entered the legislature in the Eighties were married, only five (19 percent) were either single, widowed, or divorced. No women came to the legislature via the "widow's route" during this decade.

One of the most dramatic changes in the profile of the beginning woman lawmaker in the Eighties was the significant rise in the number of women with young children. The trend in this direction began in the Seventies when the number of first-term women legislators with children under the age of eighteen increased from five (25 percent of the total) in the previous period to nine (35 percent of the total). In the 1980s fourteen (54 percent) first-term female lawmakers were mothers of children seventeen or under. Nearly three-fifths of these women served more than one term or served their first term in 1989, continuing the trend begun in the Seventies.

Though more than half of the women who entered the legislature in the Eighties had young children, the decision to combine legislative service with active child-rearing continued to be one which women considered carefully and which presented women with its own set of challenges. Carolyn Nelson of Fargo, whose children were grown, delayed running for the legislature until 1986 when she felt that the two school-age children for whom she was a guardian were secure enough for her to do so.[8] Catherine Rydell of Bismarck made her first bid for a seat in the House in 1984 when her three children had reached the ages of seven, eleven, and twelve and had "interests of their own."[9] When Julie Hill of Roseglen first decided to run for the legislature in 1982, "her two children told her with candor that they hoped she wouldn't win if it would mean transferring to a school in Bismarck."[10] She did win and the children adjusted to the biennial disruption of their school year. However, after three terms, Hill retired from the legislature to spend more time with her teenage children.[11] Diane Larson of Bismarck, who entered the legislature in 1989, described what she found to be the most difficult thing about legislative service:

"Spending so much time away from my family. Many times even when I was home I was too busy with studying to really be contributing. My family sometimes seemed to function without me, and I felt somewhat like an observer."[12]

In January 1990 Larson announced her decision not to seek a second term "citing her new job and two teenaged daughters."[13]

Occupation When First Elected to the Legislature and Educational Background

The occupational profile of beginning women legislators, which saw a two-part shift in the Seventies, underwent considerable change again in the 1980s. The shift in the 1970s had been marked, first, by an increase in the number of full-time homemakers and women employed in traditional female occupations and, second, by a broadening of the occupational profile to include students and retired persons. In terms of the first part of that shift, while the number of full-time homemakers decreased significantly (from nine to two) in the Eighties, the number of women in traditional occupations decreased only slightly (from nine to eight). A further broadening of the occupational profile of beginning women made up for these losses. The 1980s brought six women who were either employed as high or medium level administrators or owned and operated their own business, all positions which would be considered nontraditional. The decade also brought an increase (from one to four) in the number of women legislators who were students. The number of retired females remained at two.

Post-high school education, which was predominant among the women who served in the six decades before 1980, was part of the background of every woman who entered the

138

The occupational profile of beginning women legislators broadened in the 1980s to include administrators, such as Judy DeMers, who was associate director of the Office of Rural Health and director of Undergraduate Medical Education for the University of North Dakota School of Medicine when first elected. Credit: Grand Forks Herald

139

North Dakota legislature in the Eighties. Like their counterparts in the Seventies, they sought and earned undergraduate and graduate degrees with greater frequency than the women who served in the period before them. The number of women holding an undergraduate or graduate degree increased from six in the period 1923 to 1969 to eleven in the Seventies to fifteen in the Eighties. The number of women with some graduate training also increased between the Seventies and the Eighties (from two to five).

Ethnic Background and Religious Preference

The shift toward greater ethnic diversity among freshman women legislators which occurred in the Seventies slowed in the Eighties. Whereas women of German Russian, Native American, and Italian ancestry were among the new crop of female legislators in the 1970s, no women represented these ethnic groups in the 1980s. Six women represented other less dominant nationalities, including French, Dutch, and Czech or Bohemian. The other shift in the ethnic makeup of new women lawmakers occurring in the Seventies, the outnumbering of Scandinavian women by women of British Isles ancestry, continued in the Eighties. This decade saw the entry of 14 women of Scandinavian descent (or 58 percent of the total) as opposed to 18 women of British Isles descent (or 69 percent of the total). Though still fewer in number than the two best represented ethnic groups, German women continued to increase their representation, reaching 13 (or 50 percent of the total) in the Eighties.

The pattern of religious preference, established between 1923 and 1979, continued into the Eighties. While twenty (77 percent) of the twenty-six women who entered the legislature in the 1980s were Protestants (most of these Lutherans), only six (23 percent) identified themselves as Catholic or Christian or indicated no preference. During the seven decades since the 1920s, Protestants never made up less than 65 percent of beginning women legislators.

Family Political Connections and
Prior Political Experience

The major change in the pattern of family political connections and prior political experience in the Seventies was the significant decline in the number of beginning women legislators who had held elective office before going to the legislature. Whereas eight (40 percent) of the pioneer women legislators had held an elective office, only two (8 percent) of the women who entered the legislature in the 1970s had this experience. While the Eighties saw a reversal of this trend, it was modest. Five (19 percent) of the twenty-six women who won seats in the 1980s had previous experience in elective office, most commonly with a school board. Rosemarie Myrdal, Carolyn Nelson, and Beth Smette had served on school boards in Edinburg, Fargo, and Newburg, respectively. June Enget of Powers Lake had sat on the Powers Lake city council and Marie Tierney of Bismarck had chaired a government study committee in Great Falls, Montana.[14]

While previous officeholding continued to lag among would-be women legislators in the Eighties, involvement in precinct, district, and/or state party politics was never higher. Eighty percent of beginning women legislators had worked on at least one campaign and/or as a general party worker. Sixty-five percent of their counterparts in the Seventies had acted in one or both of these capacities. Service in party leadership positions on the state, district, and precinct levels saw a substantial increase in the Eighties. Whereas 35 percent of beginning women legislators in the Seventies held such a position, 65 percent of the women who followed them in the Eighties did.

Involvement in political party women's organizations, an outlet for would-be female legislators since before women's suffrage, was part of the prelegislative experience of slightly more than one-third of the new female legislators. Women

141

with this background came to the legislature in approximately the same proportion as in the 1970s. Youth political organizations, which operated as a training ground for at least three incoming women legislators in the Seventies, figured in the prelegislative backgrounds of double that many in the Eighties. For three of these women—Sarah Carlson, Connie Cleveland, and Gayle Reiten, all of Grand Forks—participation in student political organizations included officeholding.[15]

Paid employment on the staff of an elected official or the legislature, an opportunity exploited by four women entering the legislature in the Seventies, led Diane Larson to consider becoming a legislative candidate herself. Larson had been a page during the 1969 session and worked on the staff of the Senate in 1985 and 1987 before her election to the legislature in 1988.[16]

Connie Cleveland (left) of Grand Forks and Rosemarie Myrdal of Edinburg were the first two women legislators with maternal roots in electoral politics. Credit: State Historical Society of North Dakota

Family roots in electoral politics, a heritage claimed by a majority of the women who inaugurated their legislative careers between 1923 and 1979, was part of the background of half of the twenty-six women who entered the legislature in the 1980s. Although the most common family link continued to be a father or husband who had served in public office before the woman's legislative service, the Eighties brought the first female legislators with maternal roots in elective politics. Rosemarie Myrdal's paternal grandmother and her mother both served on the Loraine, North Dakota, school board. Connie Cleveland's mother, who ran for the legislature in Minnesota and lost, spent five terms on the East Grand Forks school board. Cleveland, who noted that she "grew up in an environment that naturally led to involvement at a very early age," had a father who had been on the East Grand Forks city council.[17]

Other family members who preceded this group of thirteen women legislators in winning and serving in public office included fathers, husbands, a son, a grandfather, and various male in-laws. They occupied a variety of elective offices, including register of deeds, state's attorney, county superintendent of schools, township officer, county auditor, and school board member. Three women, Julie Hill of Roseglen, Beth Smette of Newburg, and Adella Williams of Lidgerwood, had relatives who had been in the North Dakota legislature, including a husband, an uncle, and a father-in-law, respectively. Marie Tierney, who ran for the Montana legislature and lost before her bid for a seat in the North Dakota legislature, had a husband who served in the Montana legislature. When Geraldine Meyer of Berthold took her seat in the Senate in 1983, she did so with her son, Dean, another freshman legislator.[18]

Like a number of the women who preceded them, several of the women who entered the North Dakota legislature in the Eighties spoke of their political interest and

143

activism in terms of an inherited family trait. Jennifer Ring of Grand Forks became active in party politics when she was six and assisted both her mother and her father with their unsuccessful bids for legislative seats.[19] Sarah Carlson, whose grandfather ran unsuccessfully for the legislature in the 1930s, accompanied her father to district conventions before she was eighteen.[20] Rosemarie Myrdal of Edinburg, a third generation elected public official, was not the only future woman legislator inspired to become involved in politics by "political conversation around the family dinner table as a child."[21]

Organizational Affiliations

The high level of organizational activity demonstrated by the women who began their legislative careers between 1923 and 1979 was evident in the prelegislative backgrounds of the women who began their terms in the Eighties. Over three-quarters of these women were active in four or more organizations when they first went to the legislature. Like their predecessors, their organizational activity was divided among a wide range of organizations, including political, professional, religious, public service and public affairs, farm, social and cultural, sororial, and patriotic. More beginning women legislators than in the past were involved in parent-teacher organizations which corresponds with the increase in the number of women with school-age children.

The Eighties saw a reversal of the major organizational trend of the Seventies—the growing popularity of the League of Women Voters route to the legislature. Whereas over a quarter of the women who entered the legislature in the 1970s were active in the League at the time of their first election, only three (12 percent) of the newcomers in the Eighties had been League members. Perhaps other future female legislators had come to the conclusion, as Catherine "Kit" Scherber of Fargo did, that League membership "alone was an inadequate network without a party connection." She

Among the women who began their legislative service in the '80s to have a special interest in the disabled was Dagne Olsen, whose youngest son was born developmentally disabled. Credit: The Bismarck Tribune

sought that connection by becoming involved in district level caucuses and by eventually becoming a district vice chair.[22]

Legislative Interests

Between 1923 and 1979 education ranked as the top interest of North Dakota's women legislators; public welfare followed. This pattern continued in the 1980s. Nearly three-fourths of the women who entered the legislature in the Eighties listed education among their major legislative interests while nearly one-half identified one or more issues relating to what three-term representative Catherine Rydell called "human needs."[23] While the welfare of women, children, and the elderly continued to be a focus of concern, in increasing numbers, new women legislators turned their attention to the needs of the disabled. Dagne Olsen of Manvel, who was first elected in 1980 and was reelected throughout the Eighties, ran for the legislature out of a desire "to make life better" for developmentally disabled persons, including her youngest son.[24] For some of the women concern for the welfare of women was coupled with an interest in what they broadly termed "women's issues" and in specific questions such as pay equity or comparable worth, the concept of equal pay for work of equal value.

In the 1980s novice women legislators continued to emphasize a wide range of other issues. Nearly one-third of these women identified one or more health care issues as major. Drug and alcohol abuse and their prevention and treatment continued to be a focus. Legal, agricultural, environmental, and economic issues all continued to capture the attention of incoming women legislators. Of these, economic issues escalated the most. Nearly half of the twenty-six women who entered the legislature in the Eighties listed one or more economic questions among their major interests. Women commonly cited economic development and an improved climate for business as priorities.

Committee Assignments

The pattern of women's service on standing committees underwent a significant shift in the Forties and Fifties when women began to be assigned in more than minuscule numbers to committees that dealt with traditionally male issues. This shift continued in the Seventies, a decade in which the percentage of female assignments to traditionally male committees was greater than the percentage of their assignments to traditionally female committees. By the last session of the 1970s women had gained access to all traditionally male committees, including Senate Appropriations. During the Seventies women legislators continued to receive frequent assignments to Education and to the social welfare committee, though the percentage of female assignments to Education declined.

A survey of the collective committee assignments of the forty-one women who served in the North Dakota legislature in the 1980s shows that women continued to be appointed with great regularity to Education and to the social welfare committee, which after several name changes since its creation in 1939 came to be called Human Services and Veterans Affairs in the last decade. Of the twelve standing committees, Human Services and Veterans Affairs was the committee to which female legislators most frequently received appointment and Education was the third, with seventeen women (41 percent of the total) assigned to the former and eleven (27 percent of the total) to the latter. The social welfare committee maintained its first place position, assumed in the Seventies, even though the percentage of women who sat on it dropped nine percentage points from the previous decade. Political Subdivisions, considered a traditionally female committee because of its association with local government, continued to be given to women with less regularity. In the 1980s eight women (20 percent of the total) were placed on this committee.

The shift toward higher representation by women on nontraditional committees not only continued, but accelerated in the 1980s. Table 4 shows that whereas 55 percent of all female committee assignments in the Seventies were to traditionally male committees, the percentage of these assignments in the following decade was sixty-three, an increase of eight percentage points. Judiciary continued to be the "male" committee most frequently assigned to female legislators, with twelve women (29 percent of the total). State and Federal Government continued to be favorable to female representation, with nine women (22 percent of the total).

147

The most notable change in the pattern of women's representation on traditionally male committees in the Eighties was the marked increase in the number and percentage

Table 4.—Committee assignments, 1923-1989

Periods & (total No. of assignments)	No. & (%) to trad. female	No. & (%) to trad. male
1923-1946 (52)	37 (71)	15 (29)
1947-1969 (35)	16 (46)	19 (54)
1970-1979 (73)	33 (45)	40 (55)
1980-1989 (98)	36 (37)	62 (63)

of women on important fiscal committees. While there was a slight gain in female representation on Appropriations in the Seventies (four women or 13 percent of the total), it lagged far behind Judiciary. However, in the 1980s nine women (22 percent of the total) were appointed to Appropriations, making it the second most frequently assigned "male" committee. These gains were made in House Appropriations, not in the Senate. Only two (Stella Fritzell and Corliss Mushik) of the nine served on Senate Appropriations. Before to her move to the Senate in 1985, Mushik had also been on House Appropriations. Of the eight women (including Mushik) to serve on House Appropriations during the decade, three (Jean Rayl of West Fargo, Beth Smette of Newburg, and Roxanne Jensen of Grand Forks) came to Appropriations during their first term. In the House, Appropriations had become accessible to not only more women but also women with little or no seniority. The increase in the number and percentage of women on Finance and Taxation was equally impressive given the low representation of women on this fiscal committee in prior decades. Where only three women (10 percent of the total) were assigned to Finance and Taxation in the 1970s, eight (20 percent of the total) were appointed to this committee in the 1980s.

With the exception of Appropriations and Finance and Taxation, the committees with the lowest female representation in past decades remained those with the lowest in the Eighties. Transportation and Agriculture included six women (15 percent of the total), while Industry, Business and Labor had five (12 percent of the total) and Natural Resources had four (10 percent of the total). The three women who were appointed to Joint Constitutional Revision in the Eighties (Janet Wentz, Bonnie Miller Heinrich, and Donna Nalewaja) made up 7 percent of the total and were the first women to sit on this committee.

Committee Chairs and Other Leadership Positions

Between 1923 and 1979 four of North Dakota's women legislators chaired standing committees and nine served as vice chairs. Because two of these women, Rosamund O'Brien and Anna Powers, were vice chairs for two different committees, the total number of committee leadership positions that these thirteen women held was fifteen. During this fifty-six year period, approximately 2,400 committee leadership positions were awarded to members of the North Dakota legislature. Women legislators, in other words, held just over .5 percent of all committee leadership positions. Even considering that women occupied only 2 percent of all legislative seats during these six decades (123 out of 6,767), they were clearly underrepresented in committee leadership. Democratic women fared worse than Republicans, holding only 27 percent of those committee leadership positions occupied by female legislators. One explanation is that these positions are typically awarded to majority party members.

Women legislators were also underrepresented in leadership positions other than committee chair and vice chair. Only four women held a position in the hierarchy of the North Dakota legislature between 1923 and 1979. That three of these women secured leadership positions in the 1970s shows that female representation in the legislative hierarchy

During the 1989 session five women served as committee chairs. They were (left to right) Bonnie Miller Heinrich, Janet Wentz, Byrnhild Haugland, Geraldine Meyer, and Alice Olson. Credit: Doug Van Tassel. Courtesy: The Grand Forks Herald

increased during that decade; women legislators' access to top positions, however, remained limited. In terms of these positions, which each party awards to its own members, Republican women fared poorly. Only one of the four women who won other leadership positions before 1980 was a Republican. This was Minnie Craig, a Nonpartisan Leaguer. All three women who rose to other leadership positions in the Seventies were Democrats.

In the 1980s seven women chaired standing committees. Because one of these women, Geraldine Meyer, chaired two committees during the decade, the total number of committee chair positions held by this group of women was eight. Brynhild Haugland, a Republican and longtime chair of the House social welfare committee, headed that same committee for all but the 1983 session. Ruth Meiers, a Democrat, chaired it during that session. Though women had been assigned with regularity to both Education and Judiciary, no woman had headed either of these committees until the Eighties when Bonnie Miller Heinrich chaired Senate Education and Janet Wentz and Geraldine Meyer chaired Judiciary, Wentz in the House and Meyer in the Senate. The other committee Meyer chaired during the decade was Senate Human Services and Veterans Affairs. Two women came to chair Natural Resources, one of the committees not frequently assigned to women; Shirley Lee in the Senate for the 1981 and 1983 sessions and Alice Olson in the House for the 1985, 1987, and 1989 sessions.

Seven women also were vice chairs of standing committees in the Eighties. Each of these women was the vice chair of but one committee, so the actual number of vice chair positions was also seven. The most notable of these appoint-

In 1987 Corliss Mushik (seated third from the right) became the first woman to serve as vice chair of Senate Appropriations. She was only the second woman to be assigned to the committee. Courtesy: Corliss Mushik

ments was Corliss Mushik's to Senate Appropriations vice chair. Only one woman, Stella Fritzell, had sat on Senate Appropriations before Mushik, who moved to the committee in 1985, her first term in the Senate after having served six terms in the House. As only the second woman to win appointment to this almost exclusively male committee, Mushik was awarded the position of vice chair in 1987 and in 1989. Alice Olson and Dayle Dietz became vice chairs of two House committees on which women were traditionally

Shirley Lee of Turtle Lake was the first woman to hold the position of interim president pro tempore of the Senate. Credit: State Historical Society of North Dakota

underrepresented, Finance and Taxation and Transportation, respectively. Three women were vice chairs of traditionally female committees: Burness Reed, House Human Services and Veterans Affairs; Rosie Black and Marie Tierney, House Political Subdivisions. Janet Wentz served one term as vice chair of Judiciary before she gained the position of chair.

Five women held leadership positions other than committee chair or vice chair during the 1980s. Because one of these women, Corliss Mushik, served in two positions, the total number of other leadership positions was six. One woman, Shirley Lee, was interim president pro tempore of the Senate during the 1983-84 interim.[25] Lee was the first woman to hold this honorary position.

When Corliss Mushik served as second in command of the Democratic majority in the House in 1983, she became the first woman to obtain the position of assistant majority leader for either party in either house. Mushik had held the position of assistant minority leader during the 1981 session as well as the last two sessions of the Seventies.

In 1989 Catherine Rydell became the first woman to become Republican caucus chair in the House. Upon being elected to the post by her peers, Rydell described her new position as "entry-level" and commented, "I feel like I am moving into leadership roles."[26] During the same session Donna Nalewaja became the first female Republican caucus chair in the Senate.

In 1983 Patricia "Tish" Kelly, a Democrat, became the second woman to preside as Speaker of the North Dakota House of Representatives, fifty years after Minnie Craig, a Nonpartisan League Republican, became the first woman to serve in that position in the nation. Like Craig, Kelly did not wait for the position to come to her. Immediately after the November 1982 election in which Democrats gained the majority of the House for only the second time in the state's history, Kelly began "locking up her support. One week later, the media declared Kelly 'the apparent favorite' for Speaker"[27] and Kelly herself was fairly confident that she had the support of the Democratic House caucus.[28] During the legislature's organizational session one month later, Kelly secured her caucus' nomination for the position. In an

In 1983 Patricia "Tish" Kelly became the second woman to serve as Speaker of the North Dakota House of Representatives. Credit: State Historical Society of North Dakota

unprecedented move, the Republican opposition chose not to field a candidate.[29]

During the election of the second female Speaker of the House, House members spoke not only of Kelly and her new role but also of all women legislators and their roles. In nominating Kelly to the Speaker's post, Oscar Solberg, one of only two Democrats to hold that position in the past, characterized the nominee as "totally qualified and deserving of this recognition."[30] In seconding Kelly's nomination, Walter Meyer noted:

"Two of our three Democratic-NPL leaders are women. Women have a place in government and in our party, but she is being nominated not because she is a woman, but because of her high qualifications and because she has earned the respect of every member of this legislature and of those who work for the legislature."[31]

Continuing the theme in her acceptance speech, Kelly spoke of Brynhild Haugland's long and distinguished tenure in the House, adding, "I hope she and the other women who have served here during the past fifty years see my selection as Speaker as a tribute to their service to our state." After thanking her fellow House members, Kelly suggested that, "This is so much fun we really shouldn't wait fifty years."[32]

Press coverage of the selection of Patricia "Tish" Kelly as Speaker consistently noted how she went about winning the position ("call it just plain smart" wrote one reporter) and what qualifications she brought to the job ("Kelly Is Confident and Organized," read one headline).[33] Kelly indirectly discussed the subject of her qualifications when in commenting on the task ahead she said, "Confidence, competency, ability and experience with the legislative process probably prepares you somewhat."[34] Newspaper articles about the second "Madame Speaker" in the history of the state invariably made references to Minnie Craig, the first. At least one editorial called attention to similarities in the political backgrounds of the two women (specifically, their Nonpartisan League roots) and in the times in which they served as Speaker ("Depressed farm prices and a nationwide depression...").[35]

One mark of the difference between these times was reflected in the press coverage that surrounded Craig's rise to the speakership in 1933 and Kelly's in 1983. Whereas descriptions of Craig's physical appearance and her domestic accomplishments were a primary focus of articles about her, such descriptions were notable only by their absence in press reports about Kelly.

"I wasn't [seen as] 'Mrs. Housewife' and I think the reason I wasn't was that I had been in the House since 1975. I was a legislator in my own right. I had served on some very important committees—the Taxation Committee, the Appropriations Committee, the Industry, Business and Labor Committee," Kelly recalled. "I was getting to be one of the veteran legislators. And I was one of the lights in the Democratic Party as far as being a good legislator. I had that reputation. . . . And I think my press in North Dakota reflected that."[36]

Patricia "Tish" Kelly's experience proved that by the mid-1980s a woman leader could be seen in terms of just that, a leader, without having to be portrayed as a homemaker with a gavel in one hand and a dish towel or a rolling pin in the other.

Kelly's experience as Speaker of the House differed from that of Minnie Craig in other ways. Whereas Craig attributed many of her problems as Speaker to her observation that "men don't like to follow a woman,"[37] Kelly considered most of her difficulties "a matter of partisan politics."

"Probably the most difficult thing about being Speaker was that we were so incredibly close. There was

*only a four vote difference between the [Democratic] major-
ity and the [Republican] minority," explained Kelly. "The
Republicans made it a point day after day to raise challenges to how things were being run. . . . But I didn't see it
as a challenge to me as a woman, except in a few instances.
I saw it as the challenge of 'We're going to best the Democrats.' "38*

Where Craig had been frustrated in her attempts to lead by
her exclusion from strategy meetings, Kelly was able to
develop a more active leadership style. Of that style, Kelly
recalled:

*"I was very much involved. The other speakers before
that used to disappear into an office and you never would
see them. But I was visible at committee meetings. I was in
on all the strategy."39*

For Kelly, among the rewards of leadership were the
"sheer pleasure and honor of being Speaker," her proud
colleagues in the House, and her realization of "how many
young women look at me as a real role model."40 Among those
proud colleagues was Brynhild Haugland, who at the time of
Kelly's election as Speaker "told the House a woman speaker
[sic] every 50 years wasn't too much to expect."41

While women legislators made significant gains in
terms of leadership positions in the Eighties, they remained
underrepresented in top positions on standing committees
and in the legislative hierarchy. Although women occupied
12 percent of all legislative seats over the decade (98 out of
786), they held only 6 percent (fifteen out of 240) of all
committee chair and vice chair positions and only 7 percent
(six out of ninety) of all other leadership positions. Though a
woman was able to rise to one of the top two legislative
leadership positions for the second time in the state's history,
another woman, Alice Olson of Cavalier, failed in her attempt
to duplicate that success.42 While Democratic women were

157

awarded committee chair and vice chair positions with greater frequency than they had in the past, their Republican counterparts continued to outnumber them in these positions. On the other hand, while Republican women made slight gains in terms of other leadership positions, they continued to be chosen for these positions less than half as often as Democratic women.

That women legislators continued to be underrepresented in leadership positions in the 1980s was confirmed by the comments of a number of the women who served during the decade. According to Jean Rayl, who served a single term in the House in 1983, "Women are still having difficulty obtaining leadership positions." Three-term legislator Beth Smette, who agreed with Rayl, stated, "I don't think the women in the North Dakota legislature are given the leadership roles they deserve." Donna Nalewaja, one of the few women to attain a legislative leadership position other than committee chair or vice chair during the Eighties, observed that women were not "gaining leadership positions in the same time period as male legislators." Part of the problem, according to Corliss Mushik, who held a total of three legislative leadership posts during the decade, was that "women still have a hard time asking for leadership positions—some don't think they have the qualifications or that they would win—maybe feeling they don't want to get involved in challenging the incumbent leader." She added, however, "But it's a whole lot better than it was when I was first elected."[43]

Women legislators, according to Mushik, have become more assertive in their attempts to challenge what she called "the tight circle of the 'old boys' club.' "[44] That women legislators continued to encounter the "old boys' club" in the 1980s was apparent from the comments of other women. Judy DeMers of Grand Forks, who was first elected in 1983 and served for four sessions, wrote that "Women still lack the 'old boy' network which is used so effectively by men."[45] She was joined in this opinion by nine-term legislator Aloha Eagles, who said in an interview toward the end of the 1983 session, "It is harder to be taken seriously if you're a woman. You don't get into the inner circle as easily. After all these years I do have access to it, but I can't say that I am a part of it even now."[46] As a one-term legislator, Mary Kay Sauter of Grand Forks found the "old boys' club" to be "still very strong," but, like Mushik, she saw "some hopeful signs"[47] that this was changing.

According to other women legislators of the Eighties, additional problems faced the female minority by virtue of their gender. Among these were having to be "better than equal,"[48] having to prove one's credibility, especially if you were a young woman,[49] being thought of as "sentimental" and "easily influenced,"[50] sexual innuendos,[51] or, in the words of Jennifer Ring, who served her first term in 1989, "The same problems always faced by women in a male dominated profession."[52]

Sponsored Legislation

The twenty women who served in the North Dakota legislature between 1923 and 1969 were involved 576 times in sponsoring bills and resolutions and their thirty-one counterparts in the Seventies were involved 738 times. In the 1980s the forty-one women legislators were involved 1,482 times in such sponsorships. These figures show that while women legislators increased their numbers by one-third in the Eighties, they more than doubled their bill and resolution-making activity. One explanation for this dramatic increase was the carry-over of fifteen veteran women legislators into the new decade, each bringing with them a minimum of two and a maximum of forty-two years of legislative experience.

While the majority of women's legislative sponsorships in the six decades before 1980 spoke to traditionally male issues, in the 1970s the overall proportion of these sponsorships decreased nine percentage points to 62 percent of the total. Corresponding to the decrease in this category was an increase in the number and percentage of sponsorships in the remaining two categories, those that addressed traditionally female issues and those that addressed issues that affected women as a class. In the Seventies, the number of sponsorships in the former category was 225 (representing an increase of 5 percentage points to 31 percent of the total) and the number in the latter was fifty-three (representing an increase of 4 percentage points to 7 percent of the total). In the 1980s these proportions remained fairly stable, with 872 female sponsorships (59 percent of the total) that concerned traditionally male issues, 513 (34 percent of the total) that addressed traditionally female concerns, and ninety-seven (7 percent of the total) that focused on women as a class. Legislative sponsorships continued to outnumber actual pieces of legislation.

Bills and resolutions that women legislators introduced during the 1980s that spoke to those issues traditionally considered the province of men were even more wide-ranging in terms of subject matter than they had been in the previous six decades. Agriculture, election reform, licensing, and taxes continued, as in the past, to be addressed with regularity in the Eighties. The increased attention paid to individual rights and to the environment in the 1970s carried over into the following decade. Concern for rights extended to include such groups as victims and witnesses of crimes, public employees, and the interred, while concern for the environment led to legislative proposals relating to toxic waste and public transportation. The heightened priority of economic development was reflected in numerous bills and resolutions, including several designed to stimulate business by allowing the opening of businesses on Sunday, the sale of alcoholic beverages on Sunday, and the operation of a state

Mary Kay Sauter (left) and Elaine Vig, both of Grand Forks, were among the women legislators serving in the '80s whose interest in international affairs was reflected in their legislative sponsorships. Credit: State Historical Society of North Dakota

lottery and other types of games of chance. The attention of women legislators turned with greater frequency to the world beyond the borders of North Dakota as they put forward legislation dealing with such issues as representation of the District of Columbia in Congress, investments in the Republic of South Africa, the release of American hostages in Iran, and the establishment of a National Academy of Peace and Conflict Resolution. Concern over the image that North Dakota projected to this larger world led to a female-sponsored Senate concurrent resolution that urged Congress to allow the state to change its name to the more temperate sounding "Dakota."

Female-sponsored legislation that concerned the four policy areas conventionally viewed as being of particular interest to women—health, welfare, education, and chil-

161

dren—were not only more numerous, but also more inclusive. Health care and safety-related legislation expanded to include the mandatory use of child restraint devices and seatbelts in motor vehicles, the health insurance needs of uninsured and underinsured persons, the governmental and societal impact of the incidence and cost of organ transplants, the delivery of in-home health care services, and the rights of the terminally ill to control decisions regarding the use of life-sustaining treatments. Two of the major trends in welfare-related legislation were the increased attention paid to the needs and rights of the disabled, particularly the developmentally disabled, and the growing emphasis on alternatives to long-term institutional care for elderly and disabled persons. In addition, a broader range of educational issues involved classroom use of electronic media, such as satellite dishes, cable and public television, and video cassettes, the teaching of sex education in public schools, the special needs of gifted students, the use of corporal punishment, the privacy rights of both teachers and students, and the right of parents to choose home-based instruction or instruction in nonapproved private schools for their school-aged children. The confidentiality of records and information related to services provided to minors, the visitation rights of grandparents of unmarried minors, and the placement of age limitations on participation in games of chance became the "new" issues of child-related legislation.

In the 1970s and again in the 1980s, 7 percent of women-legislator sponsorships addressed issues that affected women as a class in their roles as mothers, wives, and homemakers and in their positions in the workplace, in government, and in education. The pieces of legislation in this category numbered thirty in the Seventies and fifty-six in the Eighties. As North Dakota's women legislators doubled their bill and resolution-making activity in the last decade, they also nearly doubled the number of pieces of legislation that they put forward on behalf of women as a class.

Forty-one of the fifty-six pieces of legislation that affected women as a class concerned women in their roles as wives, mothers, and homemakers. As in the previous decade, they spoke to a wide range of topics from marital property rights, to insurance coverage for mammogram examinations, to domestic violence. "New" issues continued to emerge, most notably surrogate motherhood.

The primary piece of female-sponsored legislation that dealt with the legal status of women in marriage was Janet Wentz's 1985 resolution directing the Legislative Council to study the effects of a Uniform Marital Property Act and the state's existing marital property laws. When the Legislative Council sponsored such an act during the following session, testimony in favor of the bill indicated that this legislation "would assure recognition of North Dakota women as full economic partners in marriage" and that it would recognize and acknowledge *"finally,* the contribution to a marriage by a spouse—usually a woman—who does not work outside the home."[53]

Fifteen pieces of legislation concerned the legal status of women at widowhood and at divorce. Division of marital property and support of children and the former spouse was the subject of most of this legislation, all of which sought to provide economic protection for vulnerable parties at divorce. Legislation concerning the status of children whom a divorce action might affect dealt with not only the issue of support and its enforcement but also custody, residency, and visitation. Three pieces of legislation, which Corliss Mushik and Alice Olson co-sponsored, addressed the need for counseling and training of displaced homemakers. In 1987 Catherine Rydell's bill sought to reform the probate law as it related to failure to provide by will for a surviving spouse.

Though much of this legislation was not gender specific in its language, it tended to affect women more than men because the woman traditionally has been the more vulnerable party at the time of a divorce or a death, and the mother is more frequently the custodial parent when a family separates because of divorce. The same is true of a series of bills and resolutions that dealt with the subject of abuse and neglect. Eight prospective acts addressed the issue of domestic violence, including programs and protection for victims of domestic violence, procedures for handling incidents of domestic violence, the consideration of evidence of domestic violence in determining rights to custody and child visitation, and the confidentiality of spouse abuse program records. While none of these bills referred specifically to women, they impacted women to a greater extent than they did men in that women make up the majority of victims of domestic violence. In 1989 96 percent of those who sought services from domestic violence crisis intervention programs were women.[54] A comparable situation exists with six pieces of legislation that focused on the abuse, neglect, and exploitation of adults outside of what is defined as domestic violence. Most people in need of protection and other services due to this type of abuse are the elderly. Because more women than men are part of the elderly population, they are more often the ones in need of these particular services.

The last dozen bills and resolutions in this group covered a wide range of topics, including several particularly controversial issues. In 1989 female legislators introduced two bills relating to health insurance coverage for women. The first, which Judy DeMers, Rosemarie Myrdal, Bonnie Miller Heinrich, Donna Nalewaja, and Corliss Mushik sponsored, required all health insurance policies to provide coverage for mammogram examinations for women who met certain age requirements. The second, a Geraldine Meyer proposal, related to maternity benefit health insurance coverage for complications of pregnancy. In 1989 Sarah Carlson, Diane Ness, and Jennifer Ring sponsored a bill that required diaper changing tables be installed in rest rooms in state buildings. Also in 1989 Janet Wentz and Geraldine Meyer co-sponsored a bill that called for the adoption of the Uniform Status of Children of Assisted Conception Act. This bill, which tackled the issue of surrogate motherhood, would not, according to Wentz, "outlaw payment to surrogate mothers or their use, but it would prevent courts from enforcing surrogate mother contracts."[55] The bill elicited some controversy and an illustrated editorial about "North Dakota's

Catherine "Kit" Scherber of Fargo was one of several women who introduced legislation addressing discrimination against women in the workplace in the 1980s. Credit: State Historical Society of North Dakota

secret weapon: Nordic Women."[56] Eight pieces of legislation raised the issue of abortion. In all cases they sought to limit the access to abortion.

Fourteen of the fifty-six pieces of legislation in this final category sought to increase equity for women in the workplace, in government, and in education. While none of these legislative proposals spoke specifically to the founding Equal Rights Amendment, two bills, both of which Rosie Black sponsored, provided for a human rights act to declare a state policy against discrimination on the basis of race, color, religion, sex, national origin, or marital status in a broad range of public arenas, including the workplace. In 1989 Catherine "Kit" Scherber sponsored a bill that sought to close a loophole in the North Dakota Human Rights Act which exempted employers of nine or fewer employees from employment discrimination restrictions.

Half of the legislation in this group targeted problems of employed women. One bill related to benefits of part-time employees and another to wages of individuals providing companionship services to the aged or infirm. Most workers in each of these cases were women. Two legislative proposals concerned the issue of wage-based sex discrimination. Despite the many Congressional and state antidiscrimination laws that were enacted during the Sixties and Seventies, in the Eighties women continued to experience wage discrimination and to be concentrated in underpaid occupations.[57] These two pieces of legislation, the first of which Geraldine Meyer sponsored in 1985 and the second of which Janet Wentz, Judy DeMers, and Corliss Mushik sponsored in 1987, sought to correct these problems through comparable worth legislation. Both pieces of legislation were motivated by the belief that comparable worth, or equal pay for work of comparable worth, "may be a more equitable method of determining wage-based discrimination than equal pay for equal work."[58] Three pieces of legislation dealt with an additional problem that women who were employed outside the home faced—the care of children and other dependents. All spoke to the growing number of families with two parents who were employed outside the home and of single-parent families, the majority of which were female-headed. Two bills

As a result of legislation sponsored in 1985 by Catherine Rydell of Bismarck, the name of the state Workmen Compensation Bureau was changed to the Workers Compensation Bureau. Credit: State Historical Society of North Dakota

Corliss Mushik, Donna Nalewaja, Judy DeMers, and Patricia "Tish" Kelly sponsored in 1987 and 1989 addressed the issue of what Mushik called "the search for affordable child care"[59] by providing for an individual income tax deduction for child and dependent care expenses. A bill which Catherine "Kit" Scherber and Brynhild Haugland co-sponsored in 1989 provided for uncompensated family leave, an issue that, according to Scherber, "is one of the most important issues to be considered in this Legislature."[60] Under the bill employees would have the opportunity to use leave to care for a child, spouse, or parent with a serious health condition with their employment and benefit rights protected. Testimony in favor of the bill by a spokesperson for the American Association of University Women focused on the impact of the legislation on women since "women are often the prime caregivers and often the sole wage-earners."[61] A bill which Catherine Rydell sponsored in 1985 sought to recognize women in the work force by changing the name of the Workmen's Compensation Bureau to the Workers Compensation Bureau.

The final bill in this group focused on discrimination against women in government, specifically governmental boards. The legislation, which Corliss Mushik, Catherine "Kit" Scherber, Catherine Rydell, and Janet Wentz sponsored, called for gender balance on state boards, commissions, committees, and councils. Mushik declared in her testimony on the legislation:

"We do not mean to make gender balance a feminist issue and it should not be. It is simply a matter of fairness and equity. Passage of Senate Bill 2410 will give notice that North Dakota has a policy of fairness and that both men and women will be active participants in the discussion and determination of public policy."[62]

Summary and Conclusion

Though their numbers dropped in the first legislative session of the 1980s after the upsurge in membership in the 1970s, North Dakota's women legislators finished the decade in a stronger position than they had ever held. Substantive changes in the collective profile of these political women were an integral part of this development.

Though women legislators continued to be concentrated in the House, eight from their ranks won election to the Senate in the 1980s. This was twice the number of the Seventies. While Republican women continued to outnumber Democratic women in the legislature, over half of the women who began their legislative service between 1980 and 1989 were Democrats. As in the previous six decades, women legislators were elected with greater frequency from the eastern half of the state. In keeping with the trend begun in the Seventies, urban female legislators outnumbered their rural and small town counterparts. The trend toward more multiple-term women legislators which also began in the Seventies persisted in the Eighties.

The background characteristics of new women legislators continued to change in the Eighties. One of the most significant was the drop in the median age of beginning women legislators to forty-three. The median age in the Seventies had been forty-seven. Legislative service had become more accessible to younger women in the last decade. It also became more accessible to women with young children. In the 1970s beginning women legislators with one or more children under the age of eighteen increased their ranks until they made up 35 percent of the total. In the 1980s this trend continued to the extent that women with young children comprised more than half of all incoming female legislators. Youth and young children became less of a deterrent to would-be women legislators in the Eighties than in the previous six decades. Though single, divorced, and widowed women continued to be among the ranks of first-term women lawmakers, the dominance of married women persisted.

The occupational profile of new female legislators also underwent changes in the 1980s. The Seventies had seen an increase in the number of women who were employed in traditional professions and a broadening of the occupational profile to included students and retired women. In the Eighties this broadening continued to include women administrators and women who owned and operated businesses. The number of full-time homemakers dropped. The number of incoming women legislators who had employment in traditional female occupations or were retired stayed about the same, while the number of women who were students increased.

Post-high school education, which had been a common background characteristic of women in the legislature between 1923 and 1979, came to dominate the educational profile of beginning women legislators in the Eighties. While all of these women attended college, over half had earned an undergraduate or a graduate degree.

The ethnic profile, which had become more diverse in the 1970s, shifted toward less diversity in the 1980s. Women of British Isles, Scandinavian, and German descent continued to outnumber women of other ethnic backgrounds, with women of British Isles ancestry retaining the lead that they acquired in the Seventies. The dominance of the Protestant religion among incoming women lawmakers, which was established in the earlier years, continued.

The pattern of family political connections and prior political experience continued to shift in the Eighties. Previous officeholding, which had declined among beginning women legislators in the 1970s, became slightly more common in the 1980s. While involvement in precinct, district, and/or state party politics at all levels was higher than ever, the most substantial increase was in the number of beginning women legislators who had held party leadership positions. Family roots in electoral politics continued to be a common feature of the background of incoming women legislators. The 1980s brought the first women who could claim female elected officeholders in their family trees.

Women who entered the legislature in the Eighties were, like their predecessors, highly active in a wide range of organizations before their first election. The 1980s saw a reversal of the major organizational trend of the Seventies— the notable increase in the number of women active in the League of Women Voters before running for public office.

Beginning in the early years of women's participation in the legislature and continuing through the 1980s, education and public welfare have been the major legislative interests of novice female lawmakers. Like the women who preceded them, women of the Eighties were interested in a wide range of other issues as well. While health care issues continued to capture the interest of many newcomers, economic issues elicited more concern than ever before.

As in the previous six decades, women legislators, both new and experienced, continued to be assigned with great regularity to committees that dealt with education and public welfare, committees traditionally viewed as female. The shift toward higher representation on traditionally male committees, which had begun after legislative reorganization in 1947, continued at an accelerated pace in the Eighties. Nearly two-thirds of all female committee assignments in the 1980s were to traditionally male committees. While Judiciary continued to be the "male" committee most frequently assigned to women, an increase in the number of women who were appointed to Appropriations and Finance and Taxation became noticeable. The vast majority of women's advancement on Appropriations was in the House.

While women remained underrepresented in leadership positions in the Eighties, their gains were substantial. Whereas only one woman chaired a standing committee in the 1970s, seven women did so in the Eighties. In terms of vice chair positions, eight women served in this capacity in the 1970s and seven in the following decade. Where women held three other legislative leadership positions in the Seventies, they held six such positions during the 1980s. For the second time in the state's history, a woman was chosen to preside as Speaker of the House. The woman, Patricia "Tish" Kelly, served her term as Speaker in 1983, precisely fifty years after Minnie Craig became the first woman to serve in that capacity. Even with these gains, women legislators held only 6 percent of all committee chair and vice chair positions during the decade and only 7 percent of all other leadership positions.

Women of the North Dakota legislature in the 1980s initiated twice as many sponsorships as their predecessors had in the Seventies. The proportion of these sponsorships in the three established categories varied only slightly. In the Eighties, 59 percent addressed traditionally male issues and concerns, 34 percent dealt with traditionally female issues and concerns, and 7 percent covered issues and concerns that affected women as a class. As a result of the substantial increase in bill and resolution-making activity, the actual number of pieces of legislation in this category during the 1980s was fifty-six, nearly double the number of the Seventies. While they continued to advance issues such as displaced homemakers and domestic violence, issues brought to the legislative agenda by their predecessors, they also spoke to "new" issues affecting women as a class, including surrogate motherhood and comparable worth.

Building on the work of the women who came before them, women legislators of the Eighties proved that they were now an established force. They did so through their notable gains in leadership positions, their continuing presence on both traditional and nontraditional standing committees, and their increased efforts at initiating legislative sponsorships.

Perhaps Ruth Meiers best epitomized the legislative woman of the Eighties in North Dakota. Meiers began the decade as a legislator from District Four in the northwestern corner of North Dakota and four years later became the state's first woman lieutenant governor. As the first female legislator to use her position and experience as a springboard to higher office, she represented the potential now within the grasp of her contemporaries. As a spokesperson for women in public life, she did not hesitate to identify herself as a "political woman" as the quote which opens this chapter shows. Nor did she hesitate to assert that women like herself, women in government and other areas of public life, were making a difference. And as she pointed out in her address that is quoted at the beginning of this chapter, they were making a difference because they cared.

In 1984 Ruth Meiers became North Dakota's first woman lieutenant governor. As lieutenant governor, she presided over the Senate. Credit: The Bismarck Tribune

Chapter 3 End Notes

[1]Eleanor Holmes Norton, Untitled Speech presented at the Conference for Women Legislators, Falmouth, MA, 17-20 June 1982, in *Report from a Conference: Women in Legislative Leadership* (New Brunswick, NJ: Center for the American Woman and Politics, Eagleton Institute of Politics, Rutgers University, 1986), 52.

[2]Ruth Meiers, "Women Make A Difference," Speech presented at the Girls' State Conference, University of North Dakota, Grand Forks, ND, 2 June 1986.

[3]Hartmann, 153-54.

[4]Center for the American Woman and Politics, *Women Candidates for State Legislatures: 1988 Election Results* (New Brunswick, NJ: Center for the American Woman and Politics, Eagleton Institute of Politics, Rutgers University, 1989).

[5]Remele, "North Dakota History," 39-40.

[6]Ibid., 41.

[7]K. J. Peterson, "Growth in number of N.D. women legislators comes to an end," *Fargo Forum*, 30 November 1980.

[8]Carolyn Nelson, "Women Legislators History Project Survey," completed 5 May 1989. Held by author.

[9]Gerry Gilmour, "Cathy Rydell," Bismarck Tribune, 23 October 1984.

[10]Lucille Hendrickson, "They call Bismarck home during session," Bismarck Tribune, 6 January 1985.

[11]Julie Hill, "Women Legislators History Project Survey," completed 22 March 1989. Held by author.

[12]Diane Larson, "Women Legislators History Project Survey," completed 1 April 1989. Held by author.

[13]Mike Dorsher, "Another Bismarck lawmaker decides against re-election," Bismarck Tribune, 17 January 1990, 4B.

[14]Women Legislators History Project surveys: Rosemarie Myrdal, completed 8 May 1989; Nelson survey; Beth Smette, completed 16 April 1989; June Enget, completed 10 May 1989; and Marie Tierney, completed 29 March 1989. Held by author.

[15]Women Legislators History Project surveys: Sarah Carlson, completed 17 March 1989; Connie Cleveland, completed 21 March 1989; and Gayle Reiten, completed 30 May 1989. Held by author.

[16]Larson survey.

[17]Myrdal survey; Cleveland survey.

[18]Women Legislators History Project surveys: Hill survey; Smette survey; Adelle Williams, completed 18 March 1989; Tierney survey; and Geraldine Meyer survey, completed 5 July 1989. Held by author.

[19]Jennifer Ring, "Women Legislators History Project Survey," completed 10 April 1989. Held by author.

[20]Carlson survey.

[21]Myrdal survey.

[22]Catherine "Kit" Scherber, "Women Legislators History Project Survey," completed 22 March 1989. Held by author.

[23]Catherine Rydell, "Women Legislators History Project Survey," completed 22 June 1989. Held by author.

[24]Dagne Olsen, "Women Legislators History Project Survey," completed 14 March 1989. Held by author.

[25]North Dakota Legislative Council, "North Dakota Senate Interim Presidents Pro Tempore, 1889-1989," 1989.

[26]Maureen Willenbring, "Rydell claims leadership post in House," Bismarck Tribune, 7 December 1988.

[27]Marcia Harris, "Kelly Is Confident, Organized," Bismarck Tribune, 12 December 1982.

[28]Bob Jansen, "Democrat Kelly Confident Of Election as Speaker," Bismarck Tribune, 9 November 1982.

[29]Harris, "Kelly Is Confident."

[30]North Dakota Legislative Council, Rep. Oscar Solberg Comments on House floor, 7 December 1982, Journal of the House of the Forty-eighth Session of the Legislative Assembly, 9.

[31]North Dakota Legislative Council, Rep. Walter Meyer's Comments on House floor, 7 December 1982, Journal of the House of the Forty-eighth Session of the Legislative Assembly,10.

[32]North Dakota Legislative Council, Speaker of the House Kelly Comments on House floor, 7 December 1982, Journal of the House of the Forty-eighth Legislative Assembly, 11-12.

[33]Harris, "Kelly Is Confident."

[34]Ibid.

[35]"Madame Speaker the 2nd."

[36]Patricia "Tish" Kelly, taped interview by author, 10 September 1990.

[37]"Minnie Craig No Candidate."

[38]Kelly interview.

[39]Ibid.

175

⁴⁰Ibid.

⁴¹Jack Hagerty, "Women 50 years apart as speaker," *Grand Forks Herald*, 14 December 1982.

⁴²"Alice Olson plans bid for House speaker," *Grand Forks Herald*, 6 November 1986.

⁴³Women Legislators History Project surveys: Jean Rayl, completed 21 March 1989; Smette survey; Donna Nalewaja, completed 27 March 1989; and Mushik survey. Held by author.

⁴⁴Mushik survey.

⁴⁵Judy DeMers, "Women Legislators History Project Survey," completed 25 March 1989. Held by author.

⁴⁶Nancy Edmonds Hanson, "Aloha Eagles: First Elected in 1966, She's Now Dean of Fargo Legislative Delegation After 9 House Sessions," *Howard Binford's Guide* 15, no. 10 (April 1983): 36.

⁴⁷Mary Kay Sauter, "Women Legislators History Project Survey," completed 9 September 1989. Held by author.

⁴⁸Nancy Edmonds Hanson, "Tish Kelly: Fargo Housewife Is Only Second Woman To Be Speaker of North Dakota House," *Howard Binford's Guide* 15, no. 10 (April 1983): 27.

⁴⁹Carlson survey.

⁵⁰Williams survey.

⁵¹Reiten survey.

⁵²Ring survey.

⁵³North Dakota Legislative Council, Janis Cheney's Testimony on HB 1049, House Judiciary Committee Minutes, 20 January 1987.

⁵⁴North Dakota Department of Health and Consolidated Laboratories, Maternal and Child Health Division, "Domestic Violence Program—Data Collection," January-June 1989.

⁵⁵Mike Dorsher, "Bill gives surrogate moms right to babies," *Bismarck Tribune*, 17 January 1989.

⁵⁶"North Dakota's secret weapon: Nordic Women," *Bismarck Tribune*, 18 January 1989.

⁵⁷Hartmann, 158-9.

⁵⁸Senate Concurrent Resolution 4016, 1987.

⁵⁹North Dakota Legislative Council, Corliss Mushik's Testimony on SB 2432, Senate Finance and Tax Committee Minutes, 24 January 1989.

⁶⁰North Dakota Legislative Council, Catherine "Kit" Scherber's Testimony on SB 2310, Senate Human Services and Veterans Affairs Committee Minutes, 9 February 1989.

[61]North Dakota Legislative Council, Marie Brown's Testimony on SB 2310, Senate Human Services and Veterans Affairs Committee Minutes, 9 February 1989.

[62]North Dakota Legislative Council, Corliss Mushik's Testimony on SB 2410, House State and Federal Government Committee Minutes, 9 March 1989.

4

Conclusion

This book has explored and examined a heretofore untold chapter of North Dakota's political history and added a new chapter to the record of women in American politics. It has striven to paint a collective portrait of North Dakota's women legislators, while shedding light on the individual careers of such outstanding female political leaders as Minnie Craig, Bynhild Haugland, Patricia "Tish" Kelly, and Ruth Meiers. The author hopes that the account of these women and how they came of age, which is summarized in this conclusion, will inspire and guide a new generation of women who may be considering politics.

The first group of twenty women served in the legislature between 1923 and 1969. The press, and presumably their male colleagues, viewed them with curiosity. They were subjected to a considerable amount of inquisitiveness regarding how they fulfilled the traditional roles of mother and homemaker.

As a group, these women were typically middle-aged, married, and without active child-rearing responsibilities.

179

They were well educated, many of them having attended teachers' colleges. Women of Scandinavian and British Isles ancestry predominated, as did women of the Protestant faith. The majority of these women were employed in nontraditional occupations, including banking, insurance, and journalism. Just under half had held elective office before their election to the legislature. Most of these served either as a school board member or as a superintendent of schools. About the same number had a relative, always a male, who preceded them in office. They were clubwomen, who participated in a wide range of political and other organizations.

Republican women far outnumbered their Democratic counterparts, as did small town and rural women their urban counterparts. Most of these twenty women were from the eastern half of the state and served in the House. More often than not, they served a single term.

This group brought major interests in education and social welfare to the legislature. They pursued a wide range of other interests as well. Their committee assignments reflected their major interests, particularly in the three decades before legislative reorganization in 1947. The committees that they were most frequently assigned to were Education and Social Welfare. In the Fifties and Sixties women legislators were appointed with more frequency to committees that dealt with subjects conventionally considered the province of men.

During this period a handful of women obtained legislative leadership positions. All but one of these women served as a committee chair or vice chair. The exception was Minnie Craig, who rose to Speaker of the House in 1933. Perhaps as much an aberration as an exception, Craig would remain the only woman to have served in this position in the United States until the mid-1950s. After winning the Speaker's post, a position she actively sought, Craig was to find herself a leader of men—men who did not, according to Craig, like to follow women. Minnie Craig resigned after her tenure as Speaker of the House, having proved that it was possible for a woman to penetrate the highest ranks of the legislative hierarchy.

The period produced another exceptional woman legislator—Brynhild Haugland. Haugland, who was first elected in 1939, served a total of twenty-five sessions in the House. For a number of those sessions, she was the lone reminder that women did have a place in the legislature.

While their legislative sponsorships covered a wide range of policy areas, the majority of which were in areas not traditionally considered "female," just under a dozen of their bills and resolutions spoke to issues and concerns that affected women as a class. This legislation included among other things the right of a married woman to serve as a guardian and the responsibility of women to sit on juries.

As small in number as they were, North Dakota's first women legislators created a foundation for the women who were to follow them. They did so by proving that women had a place in the legislature. Rarely did they have the opportunity to demonstrate that women had a place in leadership as well.

The second group of women served in the 1970s, when women emerged as a force in state legislatures around the country. Thirty-one women, five veterans and twenty-six newcomers, held legislative seats during this decade. Largely due to their increased presence, the press viewed them with less curiosity.

The women who entered the legislature in the Seventies changed the collective profile of North Dakota's women legislators. Though like their predecessors, they were typically middle-aged and married, they had within their ranks significantly more women with young children. They included for the first time a divorced woman and were more ethnically diverse. In contrast to the women who served in the previous five decades, these women were more likely to be employed in traditional female occupations or to be full-time homemakers. They were less likely to have held an elective office before their election to the legislature but took advantage of several "new" routes to the state house. Like their predecessors, they commonly had paternal family roots in elective politics and a penchant for organizational activity. Participation in the League of Women Voters led a number of these women to seek public office.

Though Republican women continued to outnumber Democratic women in the ranks of the newcomers, Democratic women were elected more frequently in the Seventies. Though still concentrated in the House, new women legislators served with slightly greater frequency in the Senate. Women who held office in multiple terms came to outnumber those with single terms and urban women outnumbered women from small towns and rural areas.

Like the women who came before them, the twenty-six women who entered the legislature in the 1970s shared a common interest in education and social welfare. Together with the five veterans from the previous period, these women continued the trend toward higher female representation on traditionally male committees. As they did so, they came to address with greater frequency "male" as well as "female" policy domains. While women made slight gains in their representation on important fiscal committees, the largely male legislative leadership still hesitated to let loose of what Minnie Craig had called "their exclusive right to handle the cash."[1]

While in the Seventies women legislators held leadership positions with greater frequency than they had in the past, they were still grossly underrepresented. The highest position to which a woman rose during the decade was assistant floor leader. While some women pointed to the "old boys' club" as an explanation for the relative absence of women in leadership positions, others noted the continued reluctance of women to seek actively these positions.

As women legislators increased their bill and resolution-making activity in the 1970s, they came to address with greater frequency issues that affected women as a class. Seventies women sponsored three times as many bills and resolutions on behalf of women as their predecessors had in the previous five decades. They continued to introduce "new" issues to the legislative agenda, including domestic violence and displaced homemakers. Increasingly, they advanced legislation that was designed to improve the status of women in the home and in the public arena.

The thirty-one women who served in the North Dakota legislature during the Seventies were able inheritors of the foundation that the early women legislators prepared for them. More numerous, more diverse, and in some ways more traditional than the women who came before them, these women raised from that foundation a framework on which their successors would continue to build.

The final group of women were the forty-one who entered the legislature in the 1980s. Twenty-six of these women were newcomers, and fifteen were veterans of one or both of the previous periods. With their increased numbers and seniority, this group constituted more of a force than their predecessors had.

The Eighties women brought further changes in the collective profile of North Dakota's women legislators. They had within their ranks enough women in their twenties and thirties to cause the first appreciable drop in the median age of first-term women legislators. A majority of these women were the mothers of young children, reflecting their relative youth. Never had legislative service been as accessible, nor apparently as attractive, to young women with children as it was in the last decade.

Even better educated than their well-educated predecessors, this group of women expanded the occupational profile of beginning female legislators to include professional administrators and business owners. To a much greater extent than the women who came before them, these newcomers held leadership positions within their political parties before running for the legislature. They turned less to groups such as the League of Women Voters for their initiation into politics and more to their precinct and district party organizations. Among them were the first women legislators to be able to claim maternal roots in electoral politics.

The trend toward increased representation by Democratic women that began in the Seventies culminated in the Eighties when, for the first time, new Democratic women legislators outnumbered their Republican counterparts. The trend toward greater female representation in the Senate collected some momentum when the number of women who won election to the upper house doubled over the decade of the Seventies.

Education and social welfare continued to be the major legislative interests of incoming women legislators. While remaining steadfast in their service on committees devoted to education and welfare issues, beginning and veteran women legislators of the Eighties came to sit with even greater frequency than their predecessors on traditionally male committees. Notable increases in the number of female assignments to important fiscal committees indicated a willingness on the part of the still predominantly male leadership to loosen their once exclusive control of the legislative purse strings.

Though they continued to be underrepresented in the legislative hierarchy in the Eighties, women sought and obtained leadership positions with greater success than ever before. Women experienced substantial gains in terms of chair and vice chair positions, winning leadership spots on such prestigious committees as Appropriations and Judiciary. After fifty years a woman once again rose to the top leadership position in the House. Like Minnie Craig, Patricia "Tish" Kelly sought and won the speakership in the House on her own initiative. Unlike Craig, she was elevated to the post by legislative colleagues who were willing to accept and follow a female leader. If the women who served before them proved that women had a place in the legislature, the female legislators of the 1980s proved that women had a place in the legislative hierarchy. While women lawmakers continued to name the "old boys' club" as a source of difficulty, at least one long-term female legislator serving in the Eighties saw an increasing willingness on the part of women to challenge that "tight circle."

In terms of legislative sponsorships, women lawmakers of the 1980s more than doubled the bill and resolution-making activity of their counterparts in the Seventies. Because the proportion of sponsorships in the three designated categories varied only slightly, the result was a two-fold increase in the number of pieces of legislation that affected women as a class. While introducing to the legislative agenda such "new" issues as surrogate motherhood and comparable worth, Eighties women increased substantially the amount of legislation that targeted the issue of violence against women.

If the pioneer women legislators laid a foundation upon which the female lawmakers of the Seventies raised a framework, the women who served in the Eighties took up the equally difficult task of building upon and refining the structure they inherited. As a group, these women put into action Minnie Craig's advice to:

> *"Post yourself first, establish your own opinions — don't be a gull. Build your own knowledge and confidence — and do it by yourself."*[2]

As the women who ultimately fulfilled Craig's vision of what a "lady" in politics could do and be, the women legislators of the 1980s prepared the way for their counterparts in the 1990s. These are the women who will play a role in moving the state's chief lawmaking body into the next century.

Chapter 4 End Notes

[1]Craig autobiography.

Appendices

Appendix A
North Dakota Women Legislators, 1923-1989

Name	Chamber	Post Office	Party*	Terms
Amsberry, Lavina	House	Wheelock	R	'29
Backlin, LuGale (now LuGale Schirber)	House	Bismarck	R	'73
Beauclair, Sister Mary	House	Carrington	D	'77
Benedict, Pauline	House	Berthold	D	'77-'79
Bjornson, Florenz	House	West Fargo	R	'79
Black, Rosie	House	Grand Forks	R	'77-'83
Cann, Kay	House	Fargo	D	'75
Carlson, Sarah	House	Grand Forks	D	'89
Cleveland, Connie	House	Grand Forks	R	'85-'87
Craig, Minnie	House	Esmond	R	'23-'33
DeMers, Judy	House	Grand Forks	D	'83-'89
DeMers, Patricia	House	Dunseith	D	'87-'89
Dietz, Dayle	House	Wahpeton	R	'79-'81
Dougherty, Nellie	House	Minot	D	'23
Eagles, Aloha	House	Fargo	R	'67-'83
Ellingson, Nettie	House	Rugby	R	'47
Enget, June	House	Powers Lake	D	'85-'89
Ferguson, Helen Claire	House	Rugby	R	'67
Fritzell, Stella	Senate	Grand Forks	R	'73-'83
Froeschle, Frances	House	Fargo	R	'65
Geelan, Agnes	Senate	Enderlin	R	'51-'53
Gilmore, Kathi	House	Bottineau	D	'89
Haugland, Brynhild	House	Minot	R	'39-'89
Heinrich, Bonnie	Senate	Bismarck	D	'77-'79 '83-'89
Hendrickson, Elynor (now Elynor Moore)	House	Grand Forks	R	'73
Herman, Jean	House	Fargo	R	'77-'79
Hill, Julie	House	Roseglen	D	'83-'87
Holand, Pamela	Senate	Fargo	D	'75
Houmann, Carolyn	House	Westhope	R	'79-'81
Irving, Terry (now Terry Wheeler)	House	Grand Forks	D	'73-'75
Ista, Susie	House	Walcott	R	'39
Jensen, Roxanne	House	Grand Forks	R	'89
Kelly, Patricia "Tish"	House	Fargo	D	'75-'89
Kelly, Sybil	House	Devils Lake	R	'59-'63

Name	Chamber	Post Office	Party*	Terms
Kermott, Marjorie	House	Minot	R	'73-'79
Kresbach, Karen	Senate	Minot	R	'89
LaGrave, Violetta	House	Mandan	R	'73
Larson, Diane	House	Bismarck	R	'89
Lee, Fern	House	Towner	R	'67
				'71-'79
Lee, Shirley	Senate	Turtle Lake	R	'73-'83
Lindgren, Mabel	House	Minot	R	'29
McCaffrey, Joann	House	Grand Forks	D	'77
McGinnis, Mary	House	Jamestown	R	'27
Meiers, Ruth	House	Ross	D	'75-'83
Meyer, Geraldine	Senate	Berthold	D	'83-'89
Moum, Dorothy	House	Ayr	R	'81
Mushik, Corliss	House	Mandan	D	'71
				'75-'83
	Senate			'85-'89
Myrdal, Rosemarie	House	Edinburg	R	'85-'89
Nalewaja, Donna	House	Fargo	R	'83-'85
	Senate			'87-'89
Nelson, Carolyn	House	Fargo	D	'87
Ness, Diane	House	Underwood	D	'89
O'Brien, Rosamund	Senate	Park River	D	'53-'59
Olsen, Dagne	House	Manvel	R	'81-'89
Olson, Alice	House	Cavalier	R	'73-'89
Olson, Nellie	House	Wilton	R	'37
Powers, Anna	House	Leonard	D	'61-'65
				'75-'77
Rathbun, Mary	House	Crystal	D	'33
Rayl, Jean	House	West Fargo	D	'83
Reed, Burness	House	Grand Forks	R	'77-'81
Reiten, Gayle	House	Grand Forks	R	'81
Ring, Jennifer	House	Grand Forks	D	'89
Rydell, Catherine	House	Bismarck	R	'85-'89
Sanderson, Laura	House	LaMoure	R	'25
Sauter, Mary Kay	House	Grand Forks	D	'85
Scherber, "Kit"	House	Fargo	D	'87-'89
Smette, Beth	House	Newburg	R	'85-'89
Stone, Grace	House	Grand Forks	R	'69-'73
Tierney, Marie	Senate	Bismarck	R	'81
Vig, Elaine	House	Grand Forks	R	'79-'81
Watkins, Cheryl	House	Fargo	R	'73-'75
Wentz, Janet	House	Minot	R	'75-'89
Williams, Adella	House	Lidgerwood	D	'83-'89

* Party affiliation does not reflect factions.

Appendix B

North Dakota Women Legislators By Session, 1923-1989

1923
Minnie Craig
Nellie Dougherty

1925
Minnie Craig
Laura Sanderson

1927
Minnie Craig
Mary McGinnis

1929
Lavina Amsberry
Minnie Craig
Mabel Lindgren

1931
Minnie Craig

1933
Minnie Craig
Mary Rathbun

1937
Nellie Olson

1939
Brynhild Haugland
Susie Ista

1941
Brynhild Haugland

1943
Brynhild Haugland

1945
Brynhild Haugland

1947
Nettie Ellingson
Brynhild Haugland

1949
Brynhild Haugland

1951
Agnes Geelan
Brynhild Haugland

1953
Agnes Geelan
Brynhild Haugland
Rosamund O'Brien

1955
Brynhild Haugland
Rosamund O'Brien

1955
Brynhild Haugland
Rosamund O'Brien

1957
Brynhild Haugland
Rosamund O'Brien

1959
Brynhild Haugland
Sybil Kelly
Rosamund O'Brien

1961
Brynhild Haugland
Sybil Kelly
Anna Powers

1963
Brynhild Haugland
Sybil Kelly
Anna Powers

1965
Frances Froeschle
Brynhild Haugland
Anna Powers

1967
Aloha Eagles
Helen Claire Ferguson
Brynhild Haugland
Fern Lee
Grace Stone

1969
Aloha Eagles
Brynhild Haugland
Grace Stone

1971
Aloha Eagles
Brynhild Haugland
Fern Lee
Corliss Mushik
Grace Stone

1973
LuGale Backlin
Aloha Eagles
Stella Fritzell
Brynhild Haugland

Elynor Hendrickson
Marjorie Kermott
Violetta LaGrave
Fern Lee
Shirley Lee
Alice Olson
Grace Stone
Cheryl Watkins

1975
Kay Cann
Aloha Eagles
Stella Fritzell
Brynhild Haugland
Pam Holand
Terry Irving
Patricia "Tish" Kelly
Marjorie Kermott
Fern Lee
Shirley Lee
Ruth Meiers
Corliss Mushik
Alice Olson
Anna Powers
Cheryl Watkins
Janet Wentz

1977
Sister Mary Beauclair
Pauline Benedict
Rosie Black
Aloha Eagles
Stella Fritzell
Brynhild Haugland
Jean Herman
Patricia "Tish" Kelly
Marjorie Kermott

191

Fern Lee
Shirley Lee
Joann McCaffrey
Ruth Meiers
Bonnie Miller
Corliss Mushik
Alice Olson
Anna Powers
Burness Reed
Janet Wentz

1979
Pauline Benedict
Rosie Black
Florenz Bjornson
Dayle Dietz
Aloha Eagles
Stella Fritzell
Brynhild Haugland
Bonnie Miller Heinrich
Jean Herman
Carolyn Houmann
Patricia "Tish" Kelly
Marjorie Kermott
Fern Lee
Shirley Lee
Ruth Meiers
Corliss Mushik
Alice Olson
Burness Reed
Elaine Vig
Janet Wentz

1981
Rosie Black
Dayle Dietz
Aloha Eagles

Stella Fritzell
Brynhild Haugland
Carolyn Houman
Patricia "Tish" Kelly
Shirley Lee
Ruth Meiers
Dorothy Moum
Corliss Mushik
Dagne Olsen
Alice Olson
Burness Reed
Gayle Reiten
Marie Tierney
Elaine Vig
Janet Wentz

1983
Rosie Black
Judy DeMers
Aloha Eagles
Stella Fritzell
Brynhild Haugland
Bonnie Miller Heinrich
Julie Hill
Patricia "Tish" Kelly
Shirley Lee
Ruth Meiers
Geraldine Meyer
Corliss Mushik
Donna Nalewaja
Dagne Olsen
Alice Olson
Jean Rayl
Janet Wentz
Adella Williams

1985

Connie Cleveland
Judy DeMers
June Enget
Brynhild Haugland
Bonnie Miller Heinrich
Julie Hill
Patricia "Tish" Kelly
Geraldine Meyer
Corliss Mushik
Rosemarie Myrdal
Donna Nalewaja
Dagne Olsen
Alice Olson
Catherine Rydell
Mary Kay Sauter
Beth Smette
Janet Wentz
Adella Williams

1987

Connie Cleveland
Judy DeMers
Patricia DeMers
June Enget
Brynhild Haugland
Bonnie Miller Heinrich
Julie Hill
Patricia "Tish" Kelly
Geraldine Meyer
Corliss Mushik
Rosemarie Myrdal
Donna Nalewaja
Carolyn Nelson
Dagne Olsen
Alice Olson

Catherine Rydell
Catherine "Kit" Scherber
Beth Smette
Janet Wentz
Adella Williams

1989

Sarah Carlson
Judy DeMers
Patricia DeMers
June Enget
Kathi Gilmore
Brynhild Haugland
Bonnie Miller Heinrich
Roxanne Jensen
Patricia "Tish" Kelly
Karen Kresbach
Diane Larson
Geraldine Meyer
Corliss Mushik
Rosemarie Myrdal
Donna Nalewaja
Diane Ness
Dagne Olsen
Alice Olson
Jennifer Ring
Catherine Rydell
Catherine "Kit" Scherber
Beth Smette
Janet Wentz
Adella Williams

Bibliography

Books

Anderson, Leon. *New Hampshire Women Legislators, 1921-1971.* Concord, NH: New Hampshire Savings Bank, 1971.

Andre, Pearl, ed. and comp. *Women on the Move.* Bismarck: *Bismarck Tribune*, 1975.

Blake, Carol, comp. *Women in the Pennsylvania Legislature, 1922-1982.* n.p.: Legislative Reference Bureau, 1983.

Brown, Mary. *Women in the Legislative Process.* Lansing: Michigan House of Representatives, 1984.

Center for the American Woman and Politics. *Report from a Conference: Women in Legislative Leadership.* New Brunswick, NJ: Center for the American Woman and Politics, Eagleton Institute of Politics, Rutgers University, [1986].

_____. *Women Candidates for State Legislatures: 1988 Election Results.* New Brunswick, NJ: Center for the American Woman and Politics, Eagleton Institute of Politics, Rutgers University, 1989.

Chafe, William H. *The American Woman: Her Changing Social, Economic, and Political Roles, 1920-1970.* New York: Oxford University Press, 1972.

Coe, Louise Holland. *Lady and the Law Books: Sixteen Years First and Only Woman Member of the New Mexico Senate.* Albuquerque: By the author, 1981.

Diamond, Irene. *Sex Roles in the State House.* New Haven: Yale University Press, 1977.

Evans, Sara M. *Born for Liberty: A History of Women in America.* New York: The Free Press, 1989.

Gertzog, Irwin N. *Congressional Women: Their Recruitment, Treatment, and Behavior.* New York: Praeger Press, 1984.

Gruber, Martin. *Women in American Politics: An Assessment and Sourcebook.* Oshkosh: Academia Press, 1968.

Hartmann, Susan. *From Margin to Mainstream: American Women and Politics Since 1960.* New York: Alfred A. Knopf, Inc., 1989.

Johnson, Louise. *Women in the Louisiana Legislature.* Farmerville, LA: Greenbay Publishing, 1986.

Johnson, Marilyn and Kathy Stanwick. *Profile of Women Holding Office.* New Brunswick, NJ: Center for the American Woman and Politics, Eagleton Institute of Politics, Rutgers University, 1976.

Kelly, Rita Mae, ed. *Women and the Arizona Political Process.* Second Arizona Town Hall, Soroptimist International of Phoenix. Lanham, MD: University of America Press, 1988.

Kirkpatrick, Jeane J. *Political Woman.* New York: Basic Books, 1974.

Omdahl, Lloyd. *1989-91: Governing North Dakota and the Constitution of North Dakota.* Grand Forks: Bureau of Governmental Affairs, University of North Dakota, 1989.

Payne, Jacqueline P. comp. *Women of the Mississippi Legislature.* Jackson: Mississippi Library Commission, 1980.

Robinson, Elwyn B. *History of North Dakota.* Lincoln: University of Nebraska Press, 1966.

Roosevelt, Eleanor and Lorena A. Hickok. *Ladies of Courage.* New York: G. P. Putnam's Sons, 1954.

Sherman, William. *Prairie Mosaic: An Ethnic Atlas of Rural North Dakota.* Fargo: North Dakota Institute for Regional Studies, 1983.

Articles

Baker, Paula. "The Domestication of Politics: Women and American Political Society, 1780-1920." *American Historical Review* 89 (June 1984): 620-47.

Boles, Janet. "The Texas Women in Politics." *Social Science Journal* 21, no. 1 (January 1984): 79-89.

Ellis, Mary Carolyn and Joanne V. Hawks. "Creating a Different Pattern: Florida's Women Legislators, 1928-1986." *Florida Historical Quarterly* 65 (July 1987): 68-83.

Ellis, M. Carolyn and Joanne V. Hawks. "Ladies in the Gentlemen's Club: South Carolina Women Legislators, 1928-1984." In *The Proceedings of the South Carolina Historical Association,* edited by William S. Brockington, 17-32. Aiken: South Carolina Historical Association, 1986.

Goss, Anna Mae. "Illinois Women in Congress and the General Assembly." *Research Response* (April 1989): 1-14.

Guttromson, Marilyn. "Historical Sketches of Major Constitutional Revision Efforts in North Dakota: 1889-1973." In *North Dakota Constitutional Convention, 1971-72: A Newspaper Account.* Bismarck: North Dakota State Library, 1974.

Hanson, Nancy Edmonds. "Aloha Eagles: First Elected in 1966, She's Now Dean of Fargo Legislative Delegation After 9 House Sessions." *Howard Binford's Guide* 15, no. 10 (April 1983): 36, 40, 46-7.

_____. "Tish Kelly: Fargo Housewife Is Only Second Woman To Be Elected Speaker of North Dakota House." *Howard Binford's Guide* 15, no. 10 (April 1983): 24-27, 32.

Hawks, Joanne Varner. "A Select Few: Alabama's Women Legislators, 1922-1983." *Alabama Review* 31 (1985): 175-201.

Hawks, Joanne V. and Mary Carolyn Ellis. "Heirs of the Southern Progressive Tradition: Women in the Southern Legislatures in the 1920s." In *Southern Women,* ed. Caroline Matheny Dillman, 81-92. New York: Hemisphere Publishing Company, 1988.

Hawks, Joanne V., M. Carolyn Ellis, and J. Byron Morris. "Women in the Mississippi Legislature (1924-1981)." *Journal of Mississippi History* 43, no.4 (November 1981): 266-93.

Kelly, Rita Mae, Jayne Burgess, and Katie Kaufmanis. "Arizona Women in the Legislature." In *Women and the Arizona Political Process.* Second Arizona Town Hall, Soroptimist International of Phoenix, 41-61. Lanham, MD: University Press of America, 1988.

Mandel, Ruth. "The Political Woman." In *The American Woman, 1988-89: A Status Report,* ed. Sara E. Rix, 78-122. New York: W.W. Norton and Company, 1988.

Maxwell, Nancy. "And They Lived Happily Ever After?" In *The Legal Status of Homemakers in North Dakota,* by the Homemakers Committee of the National Commission on the Observance of International Women's Year. Washington, DC: U.S. Government Printing Office, 1976.

Mezey, Susan Gluck. "Women and Representation: The Case of Hawaii." *Journal of Politics* 40, no. 2 (May 1978): 369-85.

Reid, Bill. "Elizabeth Preston Anderson and the Politics of Reform." In *The North Dakota Political Tradition,* ed. Thomas Howard. North Dakota Centennial Books Series, vol. 1, 183-202. Ames: Iowa State University Press, 1981.

Remele, Larry. "North Dakota History: Overview and Summary." In *North Dakota Centennial Blue Book, 1889-1989*, ed. Curtis Ericksmoen, 35-41. Bismarck: Secretary of State, 1989.

Saint-Germain, Michelle A. "Does Their Difference Make A Difference? The Impact of Elected Women on Public Policy in Arizona." *Social Science Quarterly* 70, no. 4 (December 1989): 956-68.

Severson, Lynn. "Women and North Dakota Politics." In *Day In, Day Out: Women's Lives in North Dakota*, ed. Bjorn Benson, Elizabeth Hampsten, and Kathryn Sweney, 205-09. Grand Forks: University of North Dakota, 1988.

Thorson, Playford. "Scandinavians." In *Plains Folk: North Dakota's Ethnic History*, ed. William Sherman and Playford Thorson. North Dakota Centennial Heritage Series, vol. 2, 183-257. Fargo: North Dakota Institute for Regional Studies, 1988.

Van Der Vries, Bernice. "Women in Government." *State Government* (June 1948): 127-8, 134.

Werner, Emmy E. "Women in the State Legislatures." *Western Political Quarterly* 21, no. 4 (March 1968): 40-50.

Wilkins, Robert P. "People of the British Isles." In *Plains Folk: North Dakota Ethnic History*, ed. William Sherman and Playford Thorson. North Dakota Centennial Heritage Series, vol. 2, 35-60. Fargo: North Dakota Institute for Regional Studies, 1988.

Newspapers

Benson County Press. [January 1923].

Bismarck Tribune. [January 1923]; 3 March 1929; 31 December 1932; 3 January 1933; 2 March 1951; 6 February 1959; 2 March 1967; 1 February 1971; 17 February 1977; 28 March 1977; 3 March 1978; 30 March 1979; 23 October 1980; 9, 21 November 1982; 12 December 1982; 2 August 1984; 23 October 1984; 2 November 1984; 6 January 1985; 20 October 1985; 22 March 1987; 7 December 1988; 17, 18 January 1989; 17 January 1990.

Boston Sunday Globe. 15 January 1933.

Christian Science Monitor. 16 January 1933.

Fargo Courier-News. January 1923.

Fargo Forum. [January 1923]; 11 February 1969; 5 February 1971; 29 October 1972; 26 November 1972; 24 January 1974; 5 May 1974; 27 October 1974; 8 December 1978; 30 November 1980; 12 December 1982; 10 July 1988.

Grand Forks Herald. 5 January 1933; 23 October 1972; 20, 26 November
   1972; 30 November 1973; 4 December 1974; 27 March 1975; 17
   December 1978; 14 December 1982; 7 November 1986; 19 March
   1987.

High Country News. 23 March 1979.

Mandan News. 11 March 1979.

Minneapolis Journal. 3 January 1933.

Minot Daily News. 31 January 1967; 22 March 1987.

New York Herald Tribune. 8 January 1933.

Nonpartisan Leader. [December 1922].

Ray Pioneer. [January 1933].

Walsh County Press. 15 October 1953.

Washington Daily Report. 5 January 1933.

Williams County Farmers Press. 9 January 1929; 20 November 1929.

Government Records and Publications

Department of Health and Consolidated Laboratories, North Dakota.
   "Domestic Violence Program—Data Collection," January-June
   1989.

Legislative Council, North Dakota. "House Judiciary Committee Minutes," 20 January 1987.

"House State and Federal Government Committee Minutes," 12 February 1975.

_____. "House State and Federal Government Committee Minutes,"
   9 March 1989.

_____. "Senate Finance and Tax Committee Minutes," 24 January
   1989.

_____. "Senate Human Services and Veterans Affairs Committee
   Minutes," 9 February 1989.

_____. *Journal of the House of the Forty-eighth Session of the
   Legislative Assembly.*

_____. *Journal of the House of the Twentieth Session of the Legisla-
   tive Assembly.*

_____. *Journal of the House of the Twenty-third Session of the
   Legislative Assembly.*

_____. *Journal of the Senate of the Thirty-third Session of the Legislative Assembly.*

_____. "North Dakota Senate Interim Presidents Pro Tempore, 1889-1989," 1989.

_____. "Senate and House Rules and Committee," 1947, 1971.

Tax Department, North Dakota. "Women Successful in Statewide General Elections," 16 February 1988.

Unpublished Materials

Benedict, Pauline. Telephone interview by author, 19 May 1990.

Craig, Minnie D. Scrapbook and handwritten autobiography, Minnie D. Craig Papers. North Dakota Institute for Regional Studies, North Dakota State University, Fargo.

Eagles, Aloha. "Women in North Dakota Politics." Unpublished paper prepared upon the request of the North Dakota Commission on the Status of Women, 1973.

Gothberg, Vera. Telephone interview by author, 24 March 1990.

Hultberg, Opal. Telephone interview by author, 20 October 1989.

Gruger, Audrey. Telephone interview by author, 24 March 1990.

Kelly, Patricia "Tish." Taped interview by author, 10 September 1990.

Kummer, Betty. Telephone interview by author, 25 March 1990.

Meiers, Ruth. "Women Make a Difference." Speech presented at the Girls State Conference, University of North Dakota, Grand Forks, ND, 2 June 1986.

Mushik, Corliss and Patricia "Tish" Kelly. Taped interview by author, 10 September 1990.

[Remele, Larry]. Minnie Craig Biography File, Archives and Historical Research Library, State Historical Society of North Dakota, Bismarck.

Thomas, Sue. "The Impact of Women on State Legislative Policy." Paper presented to the Annual Meeting of the American Political Science Association, Atlanta, GA, 1-4 September 1989.

Women Legislators History Project Surveys. Held by author.

Index

A

Abortion legislation, 60-61, 115-116, 166
Age, of first-term women legislators
  1923-1969, 27
  1970s, 82
  1980s, 134
Amsberry, Lavina, 29, 36, 42, 188, 190
Anderson, Elizabeth Preston, 18, 19
Andrews, John, 25
Appropriations committee
  appointment of women to, 46, 103, 148
  as traditional male committee, 43, 100
Armstrong, Ann, 76

B

Backlin, LuGale, 94-95, 114, 188, 191
Bailey, Consuelo Northrup, 57
Baker, Fred, 38
Bank of North Dakota, 50
Beauclair, Sister Mary, 74, 188, 191
Benedict, George W., 84
Benedict, Pauline, 74, 83-84, 95, 114, 188, 191, 192
Bjornson, Florenz, 90, 188, 192
Black, Rosie, 74, 82, 85, 93, 107, 109, 113, 128, 153, 166, 188, 191, 192

C

Cann, Kay, 98, 100, 188, 191
Carlson, Sarah, 135, 142, 144, 164, 188, 193
Child custody legislation, 164
Child support legislation, 114, 163
Children, of first term women
  legislators
  1923-1969, 28-30
  1970s, 84-86
  1980s, 137-38

Chisholm, Shirley, 76
Cleveland, Connie, 142, 143, 188, 193
Committee assignments
  as reflection of special interests, 42-43
  discrimination against women in, 43
  of women legislators,
    1923-1946, 44-46
    1947-1969, 46-48
    1970s, 101-106
    1980s, 146-49
Committee chairs and vice chairs
  numbers of women as,
    1923-1969, 49-51
    1970s, 106-107
    1980s, 150-53
  selection of, 49
Comparable worth legislation, 166, 172, 185
Craig, Minnie, 13, 14, 17, 22, 24, 25-26, 28, 36, 42, 44, 46, 50, 52-57, 59-60, 62, 63, 80, 106, 109, 120, 150, 153, 155-56, 172, 179, 180-81, 182, 185, 186, 188, 190

D

de Beauvoir, Simone, 127
DeMers, Judy, 128, 139, 158, 164, 166, 168, 188, 193
DeMers, Patricia, 188, 193
Depression, of the 1920s and 1930s, 22-23
Democratic NPL party
  challenge Republican dominance, 76-77, 130
  percentage of women legislators,
    1923-1969, 24
    1970s, 78
    1980s, 131
Diamond, Irene, 49, 109
Dietz, Dayle, 92, 93, 152, 188, 192
Displaced homemakers legislation, 114, 163

Developmentally disabled legislation, 146, 162
Domestic violence legislation, 114, 164
Dougherty, Nellie, 22, 24, 25-26, 27, 32, 36, 59, 81, 188
Drug/alcohol abuse legislation, 59, 111-112

E

Eagles, Aloha, 23, 39, 40, 42, 60, 73, 74, 103-104, 107, 113, 114, 115, 116, 117, 128, 159, 188, 191, 192
Education, as special interest of women legislators, 40-41, 98, 145
Education committee, representation of women on, 44, 46, 101, 146
Educational background, of women legislators
1923-1969, 32
1970s, 89
1980s, 139-40
Ellingson, Henry, 37
Ellingson, Nettie, 37, 48, 188, 190
Energy Boom, of 1970s, 76
Enget, June, 130, 141, 188, 193
Environmental legislation, 111
Equal Rights Amendment, 42, 61, 76, 98, 99, 116, 117, 121, 166
Ethnic background, of women legislators
1923-1969, 33-34
1970s, 89-90
1980s, 140
Ethnicity, importance of, 33

F

Family leave legislation, 168
Family political connections
importance of, 34-35
of first-term women legislators,
1923-1969, 37-38
1970s, 95-96
1980s, 143-44
Federal Emergency Relief Administration, 56

Ferguson, Helen Claire, 23, 30, 31, 32, 38, 188, 191
Fritzell, Stella, 77, 78, 88, 90, 91-92, 100, 104, 105, 107, 116, 148, 152, 188, 191, 192
Froeschle, Frances, 188, 191

G

Geelan, Agnes, 28, 35, 36, 50, 63, 188, 190
Gender gap, 128
Geographical distribution, of women legislators
1923-1960, 21-22
1970s, 79-80
1980s, 132-33
Gertzog, Irwin N., 25, 34, 35, 49
Gilmore, Kathi, 188, 193

H

Hartmann, Susan M., 113
Haugland, Brynhild, 18, 20, 21, 22, 23, 27, 44, 46, 47, 48, 50, 59, 60, 63, 74, 96, 106, 116, 128, 150, 155, 157, 168, 179, 180, 188, 191, 192, 193
Hawks, Joanne V., 38
Health insurance legislation, 114, 164
Heinrich, Bonnie Miller, 85, 101-102, 109, 149, 150, 151, 164, 188, 192, 193
Hendrickson, Elynor, 86, 91-92, 98, 117, 188, 191
Herman, Jean, 74, 95, 113, 116, 188, 191, 192
Hickok, Lorena A., 17
Hill, Julie, 128, 137, 143, 188, 192, 193
Holand, Pamela, 84, 85, 92-93, 95, 98, 188, 191
Houmann, Carolyn, 94, 95, 188, 192
House of Representatives, percentage of women in,
1923-1969, 21
1970s, 79
1980s, 131-32

I

Independent Voters Association, 23
Irving, Terry, 82, 88, 89, 94-95, 109, 114, 116, 188, 191
Ista, Susie, 30, 45, 188, 190

J

Jensen, Roxanne, 148, 188, 193
Johnson, Marilyn, 75

K

Kelly, Patricia "Tish", 57, 74, 78, 94-95, 104-105, 128, 153-57, 168, 172, 179, 185, 188, 191, 192, 193
Kelly, Sybil, 27, 38, 41, 47, 48, 60, 188, 190, 191
Kermott, Marjorie, 74, 88, 116, 189, 191, 192
Kirkpatrick, Jeane J., 28, 42, 43, 49, 73, 75, 109, 121
Kresbach, Karen, 189, 193

L

LaGrave, Violetta, 80, 81, 95, 189, 191
Langer, William, 23
Larkin, B. C., 50
Larson, Diane, 136, 137-38, 142, 189, 193
League of Women Voters, 40, 96-98, 120, 144, 182, 193
Lee, Fern, 23, 47, 74, 106, 107, 116, 117, 189, 191, 192
Lee, Shirley, 14, 86, 93, 95, 107, 117, 151, 152, 153, 189, 191, 192
Legal profession, as traditional route to politics, 30
Legal status of women at widow-hood and divorce, legislation addressing, 113-115, 163
Legal status of women in education, government, and the workplace, legislation addressing, 60, 117-118, 168

Legal status of women in marriage, legislation addressing,60, 113-114, 163
Legislative leadership
numbers of women in,
1923-1969, 52
1970s, 108
1980s, 153
selection of, 49, 52
underrepresentation of women in, 49, 149-50, 157-58
Legislative Research Committee, 44
Legislative women's caucus, 78
Lindgren, Mabel, 29-30, 36, 38, 189, 190
Link, Arthur A., 94

M

Marital status, of first-term women legislators
1923-1969, 27
1970s, 83
1980s, 136-37
McCaffrey, Joann, 108, 110, 189, 192
McGinnis, John, 37
McGinnis, Mary, 37, 189, 190
McKenzie, Alexander, 33
Meiers, Ruth, 74, 86, 95, 96, 98, 109, 116, 127, 128, 150, 173, 179, 189, 191, 192
Meyer, Dean, 143
Meyer, Geraldine, 143, 150, 151, 164, 166, 189, 192, 193
Meyer, Walter, 155
Motherhood
and public office holding, 28, 84-86, 137-38
surrogate, 163, 165, 172, 185
Mothers' pensions, 60
Moum, Dorothy, 189, 192
Mushik, Corliss, 74, 78, 80, 94-95, 96-97, 103-104, 107, 108-109, 114, 116, 128, 131, 132, 148, 151, 152, 153, 158, 163, 164, 166, 168, 189, 191, 192, 193
Myrdal, Rosemarie, 141, 142, 143, 144, 164, 189, 193

N

Nalewaja, Donna, 128, 131, 132, 149, 153, 158, 164, 168, 189, 193

National Academy of Peace and Conflict Resolution, 161

Nelson, Carolyn, 137, 141, 189, 193

Ness, Diane, 164, 189, 193

New Right, 128

Nineteenth Amendment, 18-20

Nonpartisan League, 23-24, 52

Nonpartisan League Women's Club, 36, 40

North Dakota Association of Realtors, 96

North Dakota Nurses Association, 96

North Dakota Education Association, 101

Norton, Eleanor Holmes, 127

O

O'Brien, Harry, 27-28, 38

O'Brien, Rosamund, 26-28, 38, 47, 48, 50, 51, 63, 149, 189, 190

Occupational profile, of first-term women legislators
1923-1969, 30-32
1970s, 86-89
1980s, 138

"Old boys club", 56, 109-110, 158-59, 183, 185

Olsen, Dagne, 128, 145, 146, 189, 192, 193

Olson, Alice, 74, 107, 114, 128, 150, 151, 152, 157, 163, 189, 191, 192, 193

Olson, Nellie, 30, 45, 46, 60, 189, 190

Organizational affiliations, of first-term women legislators
1923-1969, 38-40
1970s, 96-98
1980s, 144-45

P

Pay equity, 60, 146, 166

Powers, Anna, 38, 51, 60, 74, 106, 149, 189, 191, 192

Press reaction, to female legislators, 25-26, 53-55, 80-81, 134, 155-56

Prior political experience
importance of, 35-36
of first-term women legislators, 1923-1969, 36-37
1970s, 90-95
1980s, 141-42

Prohibition movement, 5

R

Rankin, Jeanette, 40

Rathbun, Mary, 38, 189, 190

Rayl, Jean, 128, 148, 158, 189, 192

Reagan, Ronald, 128

Reed, Burness, 74, 87, 153, 189, 192

Reiten, Gayle, 142, 189, 192

Religious affiliations, of first-term women legislators
1923-1969, 34
1970s, 90
1980s, 140

Remele, Larry, 56

Republican Organizing Committee (ROC), 24

Republican party
dominance of, 23-24, 49
percentage of women legislators,
1923-1969, 24
1970s, 78
1980s, 131

Ring, Jennifer, 135, 159, 164, 189, 193

Robinson, Elwyn, 14

Roe v. Wade, 116

Roosevelt, Eleanor, 17, 63

Rydell, Catherine, 137, 145, 153, 163, 167, 168, 189, 193

S

Sanderson, John, 37

Sanderson, Laura, 37, 189, 190

Sauter, Mary Kay, 159, 161, 189, 193

Scherber, Catherine "Kit", 144, 165, 166, 168, 189, 193

Senate
    as "upper" house, 64
    percentage of women in,
        1923-1969, 21
        1970s, 79
        1980s, 131
Sherman, William C., 33
Shortridge, Governor Eli, 19
Smette, Beth, 141, 143, 148, 158,
    189, 193
Social welfare committee, represen-
    tation by women on, 44-45, 47,
    102, 146
Solberg, Oscar, 155
Stanwick, Kathy, 75
State Constitutional Convention,
    91
Statewide offices, held by women,
    20
Stevens, James W., 19
Stone, Grace, 23, 34, 38, 48, 107,
    115, 116, 189, 191
Sweet, H. F., 52

T

Temperance movement, 18, 19, 34
Tierney, Marie, 141, 143, 153, 189,
    192
Townley, Arthur C., 23
Truman, Harry, 95

U

Uniform Marital Property Act, 163

V

Van Der Vries, Bernice T., 27
Vig, Elaine, 161, 189, 192
Vogel, Frank, 50
Voting patterns
    after suffrage, 21
    in 1980 election, 128-29

W

Walsh, George, 19
Watkins, Cheryl, 93, 114, 116, 189,
    191
Welfare, as special interest of
    women legislators, 42, 98, 145

Wentz, Janet, 74, 95, 97-98, 99,
    110, 114, 128, 149, 150, 151,
    153, 164-65, 166, 168, 189, 191,
    192, 193
Widow's route, 27-28, 83-84, 137
Williams, Adella, 128, 130, 143,
    189, 192, 193
Woman suffrage movement, 18-20
Women legislators, numbers in the
    legislature
    1923-1969, 21
    1970s, 75-76
    1980s, 129
Women officeholders
    climate of acceptance, 74
    traditional interests of, 40
Women's clubs, 18, 38-39
Women's movement, 74-75, 98, 113

Y

Young Republicans, 93